FAITH
UNDER
FIRE

Daniel J. Simundson

FAITH UNDER FIRE

Biblical Interpretations of Suffering

AUGSBURG Publishing House • Minneapolis

FAITH UNDER FIRE

Copyright © 1980 Augsburg Publishing House

Library of Congress Catalog Card No. 79-54119

International Standard Book No. 0-8066-1756-X

Scripture quotations unless otherwise noted are from the Revised Standard Version of the Bible, copyright 1946, 1952, and 1971 by the Division of Christian Education of the National Council of Churches.

GNB refers to the *Good News Bible: The Bible in Today's English Version* © American Bible Society 1966, 1971, 1976.

Manufactured in the United States of America

To my parents
Kolbeinn, Groa, and Sara

Contents

Preface 9

Introduction: On Using the Bible 13

1. The Basic Biblical View of Suffering 17
   A. The Background of the Basic Biblical View
   B. Affirmations of the Basic Biblical View
   C. Evaluation of the Basic Biblical View

2. The Power of Negative Thinking 43
   A. Why Do We Avoid the Biblical Laments?
   B. Analyzing the Biblical Laments
   C. The Value of the Biblical Laments

3. Suffering for Others 63
   A. Isaiah 40-55 and the Meaning of Suffering
   B. The Meaning of Isaiah 40-55 for Today

4. God, Job, and the Counselors 81
   Part One: Answers to the Question of Human
             Suffering from the Book of Job
   A. From the Prolog and Epilog
   B. Answers Given by the Counselors
   C. The Word from God

   Part Two: Comments and Conclusions
   A. The Central Message of Job
   B. Job's Problem with His Counselors

5. Is There Any Hope? 103
   A. Ecclesiastes
   B. Prophetic Eschatology
   C. Apocalyptic

6. What Is New in the New Testament? 123
   A. Reward and Punishment in This Life?
   B. Suffering for the Benefit of Others
   C. The Answers of Apocalyptic Thinking
   D. Other New Testament Texts on Human Suffering
   E. Conclusions

7. Comfort and Hope 143
   A. Summary: What the Bible Says About Suffering
   B. Giving Comfort to Those Who Suffer

Index of Biblical Passages 155

Preface

SUFFERING IS THE GREAT COMMON DENOMINATOR among human beings. Everyone has an experience of profound hurt and loneliness and suffering. Some are quick to tell you of their pain while others bear it alone and the onlooker is never aware of the misery that lies beneath the surface.

During the year that I was writing this book, my wife and I became accustomed to a certain response from persons who had found out the subject of my study. We heard it several times. "Well, let me tell him something about suffering." Sometimes the message came with a slightly different twist in the more direct question: "What does he know about suffering?"

This reaction to the idea that someone else was going to write about suffering illustrates three important aspects of this subject. First, *the universality of the experience of suffering*. With some persons, the pain is so close to the surface that all you need to do is say the magic word and the story gushes forth. Second, *the isolation of suffering*. Sufferers often feel that they are the only ones who have ever had to bear such burdens. When the opportunity for dialog is given, most sufferers are surprised to discover that they are not alone in their misery. And, third, *dissatisfaction with the answers* to our questions about suffering. "What does he know about suffering?" Many have been misled by so-called experts, religious or otherwise, who have too neatly tried to explain away great personal pain. There is reluctance to believe that one more attempt will be any more successful.

My interest in the questions of human suffering comes from three directions:

1. As a human being I have had my own experiences of suffering. They are both similar and different from the experiences of others. Perhaps I have not suffered as much as many others, perhaps not even as much as the average person. But I have suffered, and I have wondered why, and I have sought both words of explanation and words of comfort. In that, I am part of the human race.

2. I have been a parish pastor and, for several years, a chaplain in a large university medical center. What does one say when confronted with tragedy, pain, anxiety, death? It is not only a matter of making some sense of my own meager sufferings. What do I say to others who need a comforting word? How can I help them achieve some measure of insight and comfort?

3. As a professor of Old Testament at a theological seminary, I approach the subject of suffering from the point of view of the Bible. I am concerned with the connections that can be made between the biblical word and the pains of human life. In my present position, all of these aspects in my background come together—my personal experience, my calling as a pastor and chaplain, the discipline of intellectual analysis and scholarly research—in my attempt to understand human suffering. At this time in my life it seemed important to gather together some of what I have learned and what I feel and share it with others.

It is my hope that this effort will help close some gaps—between the intellectual and emotional (or spiritual) sides of religion, between the task of the professor and the task of the pastor, and between the ordained clergy and the concerned layperson.

There are several institutions and persons to whom I owe special debts of gratitude for making this book possible. Thanks to the board and administration of Luther Theological Seminary in St. Paul, Minnesota, for the privilege of a sabbatical year in which to think and write. Thanks to the Aid Association for Lutherans of Appleton, Wisconsin, who have been generous in their support of theological education and were particularly kind to me by honoring me with the Schiotz Award. Thanks to the good people of Cambridge, England, who received us with great hospitality and provided a stimulating environment for pursuing this study. Thanks to many students and pastors with whom I have shared my ideas and who, in turn, have enriched my own understanding.

I am particularly grateful to those friends and colleagues who read my manuscript and responded with insightful comments and support for the work that I was doing—Walter Brueggemann, Terence Fretheim, William A. Smith, Lowell Erdahl, David Gunn, Robert Meye, and Lawrence Murtagh. This book is better than it would have been without their help, though, of course, it may still not be as good as they would wish.

Above all, I thank my wife, Sally, and daughters, Susan and Ann Marie, for their constant love and support. It is easier to write of suffering when one is not too deeply immersed in the experience. And so, a sabbatical year, in a pleasant place, surrounded by loved ones, has provided the necessary breathing space, the vantage point, from which to approach this most human of themes.

DANIEL J. SIMUNDSON
St. Paul, Minnesota

Introduction:
On Using the Bible

THERE IS NO QUESTION ABOUT IT. There is suffering, evil, pain, grief, death, and depression in the world. It touches everyone's life at some point. Fortunately, for most of us, suffering is not with us all the time. But it is always there in the background—the threat of losing a loved one, the knowledge that we too shall die, chronic physical ailments that just won't go away, those monumental disasters of earthquake and storm and flood that destroy hundreds and even thousands of human beings at a time.

If God made a perfect world, then something has gone wrong. Where did the evil, the suffering, the tragedies come from? Who did it? Who is responsible? Why is it happening? When my personal world collapses into chaos, who should take the blame? Those of us who are Christian must find answers that take into consideration some of the things we believe about God—such as his love for all his children, his power to affect what happens in the world, and his sense of justice.

We will not attempt a philosophical definition or analysis of what we mean by suffering. Human experiences will provide our starting point. People know when they are suffering. Suffering is a personal experience. Its intensity is difficult for another to measure. One may suffer more from what seem to be insignificant causes than from what seem to be more severe causes. Suffering may come from physical, emotional, spiritual, social, or other reasons. We may be the victims of an unexplainable anxiety or depression. The sufferer knows that something is wrong, that things are not as they should be, and he or she searches for words that will help make sense of what is happening and give the strength to endure it.

We need help to deal with our questions about human suffering, whether they arise from our own personal experiences or our need to find a consoling word to share with others. An obvious resource for Christians is the Bible. Throughout the centuries, devout Christians have studied the Bible to see what it says about human suffering. This book follows in that tradition of going to the Bible with our deepest questions. Our major focus will be on late Old Testament texts. Since this part of Scripture is in continuity with earlier parts of the Old Testament and the books of the New Testament, we will of necessity do some looking backward and forward from those texts which are the primary focus of our attention.

Before we begin to look at specific biblical passages for the light they shed on our question, we must make some preliminary comments about using the Bible to find answers to our particular questions. There are many different ways to interpret Scripture. The Bible is quoted to support quite different viewpoints on important issues. Therefore, I should say some things at the outset about how I have approached the Bible in an attempt to discover what it says about human suffering. I raise these points at the beginning so that you will have some idea of my personal method of interpretation. We will return to these points from time to time as we look at various biblical passages.

● The Bible provides the basic material for the discussion of important religious questions. It is proper for Christian people to want to know what the Bible says when they are seeking to clarify what they believe. The problem of suffering was addressed many times by those who spoke or wrote the words in the Bible. It is to those words, then, that we will direct our attention.

● There is no single, clear-cut biblical answer to our questions about the meaning of suffering.

● We must therefore present as broad a picture as possible of what the Bible says about suffering. We will notice a development in the way Israel dealt with the question of suffering. Since Israel's experiences changed, old answers often needed modification or expansion. A new development does not necessarily cancel or sweep away all that went before. It only means that the old way of understanding does not fit so well in the new situation. But if a situation like the old one should recur, then the old explanation might again provide a meaningful and helpful word from God.

● When applying an ancient text to a modern situation, it is very important to compare the situation of the biblical people to the situation of the present day. All biblical words were originally addressed to specific persons at a definite point in time. If our own situation is like that biblical one, the chances are greater that the biblical message will apply directly to us.

● The Bible deals with the question of suffering on two different levels:

The intellectual level deals with the search for meaning in suffering. Why is there suffering? Where does it come from? The biblical writers are concerned with making some sense out of a world that was created by a good God but is now full of many unpleasant things.

The survival level is concerned with the "how" rather than the "why" of suffering. The problem is whether one can endure suffering, wherever it might come from, and still believe in a loving God. Many biblical passages deal with suffering at this level.

The Bible provides material on both the intellectual and the survival levels. Too often efforts to find the meaning of suffering have concentrated on the intellectual level only, and thus brought little personal support in the time of trial. It is only when both levels are studied together that the natural link is maintained between the scholarly study and the personal application of Scripture.

This book is written for those within the Christian faith who, like the biblical writers themselves, struggle to connect the ancient traditions of the faith to the reality of present suffering. There is no attempt here, just as there is no such effort in the Bible, to prove the existence of God to those outside the faith who find the presence of suffering to be a major stumbling block to belief in God. Rather, my concern is to try to help the believer whose faith is being stretched to the breaking point by the experience of suffering. In such times it is important to keep the dialog with God open, to bring our complaints to him as if he were still there, rather than to give up on his presence. We shall speak more of this.

1

The
Basic Biblical
View of Suffering

WHY WAS GOD DOING THIS TO HER? The word "why" was ring-
ing continually in her ears. She had not slept all night. It was all
like a horrible dream. She hoped that someone would soon come
in to wake her up and it would all go away. It couldn't be so.

Mary was going to die. It was as simple as that. When you
separate out the medical jargon and the feeble efforts by the
doctor to give some assurance, it all boils down to that. She was
going to die.

But that couldn't be. Dying is what happens to other people.
It happens to grandparents and distant relatives and people on
the news report who live in faraway places. Maybe when you get
old you can start to think about such things. But she was only
thirty-three. Her two children needed her. What would this do
to their emotional health? She remembered poor Jimmy, her
good friend in the fourth grade. After his mother died, he was
never quite the same again.

Her husband, Bill, was moving up in his job. He often worked twelve hours a day. How could he make it without her? How could he take care of the kids?

No good can come of this. It will be bad for everyone. God couldn't really do this to them. Doesn't he care about us? Does he have control over what happens in this world or not? What do you say to him, what do you ask for in a prayer? Why her? What had she ever done to him? She was a good person. She had always (well, almost always) been obedient to her parents. She was a good wife and mother. So, maybe she had an occasional evil thought, and there were a few people she didn't like very well. But compared to other people, how could she possibly deserve this? She thought about some of her neighbors and the way they treated their kids and their husbands and never thought about God or anyone else. So why was God choosing her for this ordeal?

She tried reading the Bible during the night. She thought it might help, but she couldn't concentrate. She really didn't know where to look. The Bible was supposed to have answers for problems like hers. But there is so much there. She tried Psalm 23, but it didn't seem to help much. Nothing can help. It can't be. Why her, God?

She found something about eternal life. She read it. Somehow, she had never really thought about needing eternal life. There had always been so much of this life ahead of her. And now all she could think of was that she wanted this life, not eternal life. Maybe later, but not now. She wasn't worried about hell. Hell would certainly be an overcrowded place if people whose sins were as modest as hers got sent to hell. God just wouldn't operate like that. But she wasn't all that excited about going to heaven either. She had no idea what that would mean. She just wanted to stay, to be herself, with her family. "O God, let it all be a big mistake or a bad dream."

And the pain. O God, she couldn't even think about that. Could she stand it? So far it wasn't so bad. But she knew it would get worse. She had always been a coward about doctors. She worried for days about getting shots. How could she take it? She didn't want to be a disgrace to her family. This was going to be hard enough for them to handle.

But then again, why should she have to take all this pain? Why was God doing this to her? What kind of world is this? Is there no justice? Why don't stories always have happy endings?

She couldn't sleep. She couldn't think straight. She paced the room. In desperation, she sat down and thumbed through the Bible again.

———————

What a way to end a vacation! He had no sooner come in the door when a call came about Mary. Please God, not Mary. They just don't come any better than Mary. She certainly doesn't deserve this.

There are days he would just as soon not be a pastor. To be sure, there are many wonderful days—sharing the joys of births, baptisms, weddings, anniversaries. It is a precious privilege to be able to speak to people of God's love and to share the sacraments with them and to feel their love and support. He had never been one of those cool, detached pastors. He loved to mingle with his people. They were his friends. Most of the time he could honestly say that he loved them (at least most of them). But that made the hurt so much deeper when things like this happen to his people. Mary was something special. Some days it is tough being a pastor.

What can he say to her—and to Bill and the kids? He knows their questions. He has heard them before. He has thought all of them himself—many times. But what are the answers? He is supposed to know. He is the pastor. Some days he feels like he knows something worth sharing with others. But today he isn't sure. Today is only pain and sadness and wondering what God is up to.

He knows he must go to see her. He wants to go—but he can hardly stand to go. It will be painful. He will feel inadequate. With such big hurts, anything he can say will seem so trivial.

He picks up his Bible—and his communion kit. He mumbles an almost incoherent prayer. Slowly he heads for the car. What a way to end a vacation!

There must be some reason. Suffering must make some kind of sense. Life cannot be a gigantic game of Russian roulette where anyone's chances of getting killed are the same as anyone else's. If God is personally involved in what happens in the world, if he has any influence on what happens, if he loves us as he says he does, then there ought to be some explanation for the suffering which is all too common to human existence.

"Why me? What did I do to deserve this?" The words came out of Mary's mouth like a reflex action. For many Christians, the first reaction when tragedy strikes is to think in terms of rewards and punishments. Patients in the hospital think over their past, wondering if they have done something for which they are now paying the price. Mary's friends and family shake their heads as they repeat over and over again, "She doesn't deserve this." People should not have to endure what they do not deserve. We want the world to make sense. If we must bear pain and suffering in this life, we want to have an explanation and some answers. And the answer that most quickly comes to our minds is to try to find some connection between the wrongs that we have done and the suffering that has come as a consequence of our actions.

Well-indoctrinated Christians often look within themselves for the cause of suffering. This is a common response for us, a feeling in our bones. And for good reason. We have learned to think like this from years of exposure to biblical passages which seem to make this point either directly or in more subtle ways. Further, we have been exposed to sermons, radio and TV "evangelizers," the theologizing of friends and relations, and even liturgies that have helped reinforce the idea that our own suffering is probably our own fault. This is the prayer of confession from a 1941 Order of Holy Communion: "O Almighty God, merciful Father, I, a poor, miserable sinner, confess unto thee all my sins and iniquities with which I have ever offended Thee and justly deserve Thy temporal and eternal punishment." And, in the general prayer in the same service: "And although we have deserved Thy righteous wrath and manifold punishments, yet, we entreat Thee, O most merciful Father, remember not the sins of our youth nor our many transgressions . . ." In another Order of Public Confession from 1958 the congregation is asked to give its assent to these words: "Do you confess that you are by nature a most unworthy sinner, and that you have grievously offended against him, in thought, word, and deed, and have merited only his wrath and condemnation?"

So, when people suffer and we are looking for some explanation, some reasons, some answers, someone to blame, who is the logical candidate? People, of course. It is our own fault. We have brought the suffering upon ourselves. The Bible can be quoted to support that idea and the church has provided many ways to reinforce the belief that suffering is punishment for sin.

There is no single answer to our questions about suffering. But the view that people such as ourselves are responsible for all the trouble that has come into the world is so basic that it must be our starting point. We must look at it carefully and examine a sampling of those biblical texts that seem to support it. Many people are painfully aware of this solution to the dilemma of human suffering. They should not be overwhelmed by the often harsh words we shall look at in this chapter. Though these words may seem heavy and oppressive at times, they are not the only ones the Bible has to offer on the theme of suffering.

A. The Background of the Basic Biblical View

In this chapter we will first look at some texts and then attempt to put them in perspective and give some evaluation. The texts have been chosen because they present the theme that human beings are the cause of the suffering in the world. God is also a participant in these texts; he sees to it that good and evil come to the right people, depending on their relationship to him and to other people.

We will look at these texts in roughly chronological order, beginning with texts originating in prosperous times and moving to those coming out of a time of national disaster. There is a movement in these texts from a general principle to a gradually more specific application—from an explanation of the state of *humankind in general* to an interpretation of specific historical events in the life of the *whole people* to an explanation of particular incidents in the lives of *individual persons*. The belief in retribution (as this view is often described) becomes more unsatisfactory as it is applied more particularly. As we shall see, if we pick it up only at this last level, as a way of explaining specific sufferings of individual people, we will face many hazards.

Our look at those texts that have shaped our belief in the doctrine of retribution will be brief. We can attempt no detailed interpretation. We shall introduce some of the most important texts, make a few observations and comments, and then invite your further reflections. We have divided the texts into four classifications—(1) the story of the Fall, (2) motivation for ethical behavior, (3) interpretations of Israel's history by historians and prophets, and (4) application to events in individual lives.

1. The story of the Fall

Genesis 3 is perhaps the most significant passage in the entire Bible on the meaning of human suffering. This is the story of the coming of evil into the world. The claim has been made in Genesis 1 that the world is good and that God took special delight in what he had made. Some transition is necessary to move from the idyllic picture of Eden in Genesis 2 to the reality of the world as it has been known throughout history. What went wrong? Genesis 3 attempts some answers.

A story like this is subject to varied interpretations. Christians have discussed its precise meaning for centuries. Briefly, we can say this much with regard to our questions about human suffering:

• God did not bring the suffering. He made a good world and intended it to remain that way.

• The human beings—both the man and the woman—are responsible for bringing pain and suffering into the world. Their act of disobedience triggers all the disasters that follow. The ensuing stories in Genesis 4-11 emphasize the desperate situation of humanity and the need for some kind of saving action on God's part (which begins with the calling af Abraham). The deeper implications, however, reveal a profound description of the human situation. We are not content with our human limitations. As long as we continue to trust God and believe his word to us, we can live with the uncertainties of being human. But when we wish to be like God so that we do not need to rely on him, the result is alienation, distrust, sin, and the terror of being a limited human without the support of a trusting relationship with God.

• The presence of the snake in Genesis 3 is very significant. It introduces an element of mystery into this explanation of the origin of evil. Though the primary responsibility seems to lie with humans, and it certainly does not lie with God, there is some strange presence outside ourselves which entices us into the kind of behavior that is going to get us in trouble. The snake is not the devil, as the devil is later understood. Neither is he identified as Satan, though his function is like Satan and later tradition identifies him with Satan. His presence helps take a little of the edge off the conclusion of the story—human beings are responsible for the evil that comes into the world. That statement is still true, but the presence of the snake allows some open-endedness, some flexibility, some doubt whether this principle can be applied in an absolute sense to every specific example of human suffering. Evil seems almost bigger than something that human beings can bring about by themselves.

This is a story about beginnings, an explanation of how this world came to be the way it is. The dating of this story is very uncertain. Many scholars believe it was written during the monarchy of David and Solomon. This was a fairly optimistic, prosperous era in Israel's history. But even in the best of times, there is evil and suffering and death which require some word of explanation.

2. Motivation for ethical behavior

Many biblical texts promise good things to those who obey God's commands and unpleasant consequences to those who disobey. These biblical passages have had a profound influence on us and have conditioned our belief that suffering is the result of our own sins. Those of us who are religious have a large investment in the truth of this belief since we have opted for a life of obedience. We are bothered if "good" people seem to have more than their share of suffering, but we are also bothered by "bad" people who have things going too well. If the idea of retribution does not work, then there is fear that the motivation for ethical behavior will disappear.

Some examples of texts that fit this category are:

Exodus 34:6-7 (with parallels though not identical in Exodus 20:5-6, Deuteronomy 5:9-10, and Numbers 14:18).

> The Lord passed before him and proclaimed, "The Lord, the Lord, a God merciful and gracious, slow to anger, and abounding in steadfast love and faithfulness, keeping steadfast love for thousands, forgiving iniquity and transgression and sin, but who will by no means clear the guilty, visiting the iniquity of the fathers upon the children and the children's children, to the third and fourth generation."

There is a definite connection between the evil acts of people and the unfortunate consequences of those acts. And it goes beyond our individual sins and punishments. What our ancestors did has already determined some of our problems, and what we are doing will have its ill effects on our own children and grandchildren. There is a continuity, a vicious circle, to this whole unpleasant business. It seems impossible to get out of it.

Yet there appears to be some opportunity for choice, in spite of the legacy left by our forebears. This particular passage occurs in the context of the Ten Commandments in both Exodus 20 and Deuteronomy 5, as well as in another legal code in Exodus 34. The intention is to impress on God's people that they are expected to be obedient. They have a choice, but they should know that they cannot make the wrong choice without facing certain consequences.

Deuteronomy 5:11 and 16

Two of the Ten Commandments speak about the consequences of obedience or disobedience. God will not hold guiltless the one who takes his name in vain, and God will prolong the days and make things go well for the ones who honor father and mother. We have learned the Ten Commandments and these words have become part of our religious belief. Life should go well for good people and evil doers should expect problems.

Deuteronomy 28

The whole Book of Deuteronomy has a hortatory, sermonic style. The law is not simply recited and left as an abstraction which one can decide to accept or reject. Rather, the book is filled with promises of good fortune or dire warnings of doom, depending on one's response to what God demands. Deuteronomy reaches a climax in Chapters 27 and 28 in a series of blessings and curses that are apparently recited in a ceremony in which Israel renews her covenant with her God. The connection between our ethical behavior and the good or bad that happens to us is clearly presented. Those ancients really knew how to curse. They almost seemed to enjoy the curse more than the blessing. Curses outnumber blessings, and the imagery is terrifyingly detailed.

As one reads through the blessings and curses of Chapter 28, special attention should be paid to verse 35: "The Lord will smite you on the knees and on the legs with grievous boils of which you cannot be healed, from the sole of your foot to the crown of your head." Is there any wonder that Job's counselors assumed that Job's physical problems were a result of being cursed for some sin he had committed?

Deuteronomy 30:15-20

This is a good summing up statement of the theology of the Book of Deuteronomy and probably the dominant view of most people in Israel up to the time of the exile. God has set a choice in front of his people. They can choose life and good, or death and evil. If they choose the former all will go well and they will be able to live long and prosperously in their land. If they choose the latter they will perish and not last long in their promised land. We should note that God is urging them to make the correct choice. He does not want anyone to perish. Nevertheless, if they insist on being disobedient, they have no one to blame but themselves. They have been warned.

These are not favorite passages for most people. But they are there in the Bible. We know about them. We understand the theology presented by them—human beings bring misfortune and suffering upon themselves by the way they live.

3. Interpretations of Israel's history

There is another group of biblical texts that supports the same view as the exhortations about moral behavior listed above. These are texts in which the writer, whether telling the history of the people or prophesying impending doom, assumes a natural link between the sins of the people and the specific events which either have occurred or soon will occur. The Bible contains many examples of this, but they are especially prominent in the great historical work of Joshua, Judges, Samuel, and Kings and in the oracles of the pre-exilic prophets. Here are a few examples:

Joshua 7

The story of the sin of Achan and its consequences is one of the more difficult Old Testament stories for Christians to accept and from which to find an uplifting message. Achan keeps for himself some of the booty that was meant to be dedicated to the Lord. As a result of the sin of one man, things go badly for the whole people in their subsequent battles. When Achan is found out, drastic action is taken to remove not only Achan himself but his whole family from the society.

In this story, it is assumed that disasters come from human sin. It is important to note that the sin of one individual can have far-reaching effects. That means that the suffering I am enduring may be the result of someone else's sin, not just my own. No one lives entirely to oneself. What we do has its effects on others and vice versa. The belief that evil deeds have their consequences is upheld, but in this example it is not extended to explain that every *individual's* suffering is necessarily the fault of that individual. Achan's family did not sin as individuals, but they are still guilty and liable to punishment as part of a family.

Judges 2:6-23

The historian who collected stories about the time of the judges has the same view of the meaning of suffering as we have been outlining in this chapter. He assumes that there are discernible cause and effect relationships between what people do and what happens to them. In this passage, before he starts to tell of the escapades of individual judges, he tells us that there is a general pattern that fits the story of each of the judges. The people were not faithful to God so he sent them an enemy to torment them.

Finally, when the people would cry to God for help, he would send them a deliverer, a judge, who would defeat the enemy. Things would go well until the judge died, then the people would backslide, God would send another enemy, and the whole cycle would be repeated. The historian interprets the fluctuating fortunes of the tribes of Israel as being the result of their lack of faithfulness to God.

2 Kings 17

This chapter tells of the end of the northern kingdom of Israel. Further, we are told why this happened: "And this was so, because the people of Israel had sinned against the Lord their God, who had brought them up out of the land of Egypt from under the hand of Pharaoh king of Egypt, and had feared other Gods" (verse 7). The chapter goes on to explain in greater detail how all this came about.

The suffering, the evil, the destruction that comes to the northern kingdom is explainable. We can point to a variety of misdeeds and say that these are the reasons that the calamity occurred. The general doctrine of human beings causing their own suffering is applied to specific historical situations. There is a boldness on the part of the historian. At least in this particular instance of large-scale suffering, he is able to tell us why it happened.

Amos 2:6-7, 13-16; 4:11-12; 5:14-15; 6:14

All the great pre-exilic prophets (Amos, Hosea, Isaiah, Micah) started with the same assumptions. The impending doom is a result of the sins of the people, particularly those of the leaders in government, business, and religion. The prophet is sent by God to warn the people of what is coming. Some of the prophets assume that it is already too late for repentance, even if the people would pay attention to what they are saying. But, whether their word is heeded or not, at least later generations will know why God did this to them. They will know that God had not abandoned them, or acted arbitrarily, or failed in some show of power. God had in fact been faithful to his end of the covenant. The people brought it on themselves by their sin, even though God had tried to head them off by warning them of the consequences. He had given them laws, he had sent historians who interpreted past events as warnings not to let history repeat itself, and he sent the prophets.

Amos and the other great prophets made direct connections between the sins of the people and the horrible events which they saw so clearly before anyone else could see them. Human beings bring their own troubles on themselves. If you live in a society that breaks its covenant with God, then you better expect the worst.

4. Application to events in individual lives

In our choice of texts, we began with the general statement about the coming of evil and suffering in the world. Then we looked at the use of the concept of retribution as a motivation for obeying God's law. Next we saw examples of how this principle was used to make sense out of specific events in the life of the people.

In Ezekiel, we see a new emphasis. It is in continuity with the old doctrine, but it tries to extend it in a new direction. Ezekiel 18 is the basic material for our consideration of this switch in emphasis.

Ezekiel lived at the time of the destruction of Jerusalem, the great calamity prophets had anticipated but which had seemed impossible to most good citizens of Judah. Ezekiel spoke before the disaster came, warning of its inevitability. He also spoke after the exile began, changing his word from gloomy predictions to a more appropriate expression of hope. Chapter 18 is apparently set during the exile—at any rate, it gives the impression that things have been going badly for some time.

Ezekiel responds to a proverb that has been floating around among the disillusioned young people who have had their future taken away from them by the national calamity. (Jeremiah responds in a different way to the same proverb in Jeremiah 31:29-30.) The proverb says, "The fathers have eaten sour grapes, and the children's teeth are set on edge." The proverb is expressing a bitter sense of injustice by younger people because their fathers committed the sins for which they are now being punished. "Why should we suffer for what our parents and grandparents did? Why didn't God punish them? What is the point of picking on us who were either not born or were too young to be responsible when all these so-called sins were taking place?"

Those young people knew that the historians and prophets interpreted the exile as God's punishment. They no doubt also knew those passages about the sins of the fathers being passed on to the third and fourth generations. And they didn't like it.

Ezekiel's response is very interesting. He says (v. 4), "Behold, all souls are mine; the soul of the father as well as the soul of the son is mine: the soul that sins shall die." And in verse 20, "The soul that sins shall die. The son shall not suffer for the iniquity of the father, nor the father suffer for the iniquity of the son; the righteousness of the righteous shall be upon himself, and the wickedness of the wicked shall be upon himself." If the wicked repent, they will live. If the righteous fall away, they will die. One cannot be punished for the sins of one's ancestors; neither can one be saved by the virtues of an ancestor. Everyone is on his or her own, to sink or swim. God is just and will respond to individuals precisely on their own merit. (See also Deuteronomy 24:16.)

We have here an individualizing of the principle of retribution. It is surely an overstatement on the part of Ezekiel. At least it is not meant to be a general principle that can explain the good or ill fortune of every individual life. It seems to deny the interdependence of a society, a belief which was so significant in the warning about the sins of the fathers and their pervasive effect. It pushes the retribution principle to a point where it is difficult to make it correspond with actual experience, at least as long as we are still talking about appropriate compensation in this life (which Ezekiel seems to be doing) and not opening the door to a recompense in some future life.

We shall say a bit more about the strengths and the weaknesses of Ezekiel's understanding of the meaning of suffering at the end of this chapter. Suffice it to say that, with the spread of individualism in the Western world, the position expressed by Ezekiel has had a wide acceptance.

These examples present what I have called the basic biblical answer to the question of human suffering. According to these passages, human beings bring misfortune on themselves as a result of their sin. Further, it is possible to discern connections between specific sins and the results, especially when talking in more general terms about all of humanity or interpreting the fortunes of a specific society. Some would say (as Ezekiel) that one can even see such connections in the lives of individuals.

The Bible does say this, in a very prominent way. It is a point of departure for our study of human suffering. But how directly can we, or should we, apply the message of these passages to our contemporary search for answers to this most persistent question? Let us open that discussion in two ways. First, I will list some points about God and the world that are being affirmed by the basic biblical view. Second, let us see if this view can adequately explain all human suffering.

B. Affirmations of the Basic Biblical View

1. God is personal

The basic biblical view presents to us a God who is personal, who is concerned, and who actively participates in what happens in the world. One can speak, as these texts do and as Christians often do, of the things that God has done in the life of his people. God is not remote and far off. As he was involved with human beings in biblical times, so he is today.

When we try to be more specific about the way God involves himself in the events of the world, we find a wide range of opinion, both with regard to the understanding of the biblical texts in their original setting and with regard to their meaning in our contemporary world. For example, does God actually bring rewards and punishments into our lives? Does he pull strings and push buttons and send bacteria and cause cancer? Is his involvement that direct? What does it mean to say that God punishes us through the deeds of someone else (like the burglar who ransacked our house or the garage mechanic who forgot to tighten the bolt or the neighbor who hates children)? Does God allow them to do such things or is it possible that many unpleasant things are not really directly under God's control at all? Some would like to believe in an orderly world, created by God, in which there is a natural link between what we do and the results that eventually emerge from those deeds. We have been told how we should live and, if we refuse, then we ought not be too surprised when unpleasant things happen to us—it is inevitable. This still allows for God's involvement in the world and for the consequences of our behavior, without making God into a meddler who controls every minute of every person's life.

However we attempt to make sense of God's activity in the world, these texts we have been examining affirm the belief that he is present and concerned and will ensure that eventually everything will work out as it should.

2. God is just

God is not frivolous. He is not arbitrary. He is not evil. He cares how we treat one another and he wants everyone to be treated fairly. Therefore, certain sanctions are attached to his laws. They cannot be disobeyed with impunity. There is a price. His justice demands it as protection for the weak and helpless. There is good reason for the law and there is reason for the dire results that follow the breaking of the law.

3. Humans have a choice

The exhortations in Deuteronomy, the biblical historian in Judges, the prophets like Amos and Ezekiel all assume that people can choose rightly or wrongly in key situations. It is not inevitable that we will always make the wrong choice. If the alternatives and consequences are clearly stated, the hope is that people will choose rightly. There are gradations of right and wrong. We ought not wash away all human decisions in a doctrine of original sin that defines all human actions as sinful, and therefore removes the need for discrimination and good judgment in making human decisions.

In the passage about the "sins of the fathers" and in the despair of some prophets that it is already too late for repentance, we have at least the hint that humans may be incapable of making correct choices. Nevertheless, this aspect is not pushed to the point of obliterating the importance of human freedom.

4. There is order in the world

The world does have order. It makes sense. We can study it and learn from it. Cause and effect relationships do exist. They can be discovered, and this information can be useful as we make decisions that shape what happens to us and our society. By so doing, it is even possible to make a better world.

5. We need evidence of God's justice

God's justice must be seen in *this world*. None of the passages we have mentioned so far assumes a belief in the next world to alleviate the need to explain the suffering in this world. There is almost a frantic need to have good things come to the righteous and bad things to the wicked in this life because there is no other life. This leads to a heightened sense of responsibility and social awareness. One cannot put off the search for justice, the need to right a wrong, the hard questions of what God is doing.

This is a strength, in a way, because it never backs away from real human pain to offer "pie in the sky." It, of course, is also a weakness, especially as applied by Ezekiel to the life of an individual. There is no way that people are always compensated according to their deserts *in this life.*

6. Our existence is corporate

There is a corporate aspect of our existence. We are constantly inter-relating with one another and what another person does has its effect on me. I may suffer because of something you do, even if you do not intend to hurt me, or are, perhaps, not even aware of my existence. It is foolish to apply the concept of retribution in such individual ways that we fail to take into account our relationships with one another. This is true across generational lines, as so well stated in Exodus 34:6-7 and parallels, and it is true for ourselves and our contemporaries.

It would be an oversimplification to say that I suffer from certain anxieties or that I have a bad case of myopia because of some sins I have committed. If you look into my family tree, you will find some of the same psychological problems, and the same bad eyes present in many previous generations. If someone sinned to start all of this off, it is too far back to locate. We are related to each other across generational lines and all our suffering cannot be directly connected to our individual sins.

A young man killed by a drunken driver is a tragic event. It is ludicrous to try to understand such a disaster in highly individualized terms—that is, as if the young man deserved what happened to him. But, in a larger social sense, it may make some sense. We live in a society that influences some persons into alcoholism, and we ought not be too surprised when the suffering that follows touches apparently innocent lives. All of us suffer, not just the alcoholic.

We have thought about ourselves as individuals, somehow insulated from the world around us, for so many centuries now that it is hard for us to recover that sense of corporateness expressed in these early biblical texts.

These are some of the affirmations about God and his relationship to the world based on the biblical passages examined so far. Some of these are points we would still want to maintain. Though we may be disillusioned with the principle of retribution, we ought not to assume that all these passages are outdated and no longer applicable. The idea that humans bring about their own suffering remains the basic biblical view and all later biblical discussion must begin here.

C. Evaluation of the Basic Biblical View

1. Strengths

● This view really does work most of the time. It is true that we reap what we sow. Much of our suffering is brought about by our inability to live in loving relationships with God and with one another. It may be that we even bring many physical illnesses on ourselves by our unhealthy life-styles, our polluted air, our doctored food. We do not cause earthquakes or floods, but we build cities in places that we know are vulnerable to these catastrophes. There may be many more connections between our choices and the sufferings of life that we don't even know about.

● The world does have order and meaning. Problems can be analyzed and solutions sought. The world can be better.

A common complaint in our day is that the world makes no sense. There seems to be no pattern, no meaning, no ethical guidelines. We see no cause-and-effect relationship between behavior and life. The old standards are threatened and no one knows whether they are important enough to maintain or not.

In such a meaningless and wishy-washy world, the message of Deuteronomy may have an appropriate place again. Our decisions have consequences that are often predictable. When you live a life without loving others, you will live a lonely life in which others do not love you. We cannot act with impunity and do whatever we please without some day having to answer for it. And the unfortunate results may well come within this world, and not only as a threat for punishment in some future world.

● Forgiveness does not come cheaply. The power of forgiveness to open new doors and make healing possible is immense. But no amount of forgiveness can immediately wipe away all the effects of years of hurting other people. For example, a man who has been an alcoholic for 15 years finally sinks to the depths, turns himself over to a higher power, joins the AA, becomes a useful and helpful citizen, and never touches a drop again. He has been forgiven. He is now living a new life. It is possible. But, the effects of those 15 years on his family continue to exert their influence. His wife and children have forgiven him, but their lives have been so shaped by their experience of living with him that they cannot forget the past and live as if it had not happened. Their lives will continue to be filled with more sadness, more anxiety, more suffering than would be the case if their father had joined AA 15 years earlier. His life is certainly better now, but, in a sense, it is too late for them.

This view of suffering faces reality head-on. It does not back off from human pain. It does not put the responsibility on someone or something out there, but puts it right back on people where it belongs. There is certainly some value to that message, if it is directed to people who actually could benefit from hearing a hard word like that.

The word of Ezekiel could also be liberating in some cases. The balance between corporate and individual responsibility for our troubles is a very delicate one. On the one hand, we can take personal responsibility for everything—even for the decisions of the President of the United States, despite the fact that we voted against him every time he ran. On the other hand, we can refuse to accept any responsibility for ourselves and our own actions. It is all someone else's fault.

For those who think all their troubles are caused by someone else, Ezekiel has a message. For those young people who blame the adult world and all its institutions and attitudes for their own problems, but see no fault of their own and no hope of change, Ezekiel can be an appropriate word. For the person who has been in psychoanalysis for years and is still trying to clarify what his mother did to enslave him, for the ghetto dweller who has hundreds of years of neglect and discrimination to overcome, Ezekiel offers a message of hope.

So there is some positive value to this biblical view, even without the refinement of future biblical insight which will qualify it in a number of ways. There are occasions when this hard word of cause-and-effect relationships and the centrality of human responsibility can be an authentic word from God.

There are problems, however, if this view is accepted as a universal explanation for suffering.

2. Weaknesses

• It does not explain everything. As we have said, there is no single biblical answer that can explain every instance of human suffering. The idea that human beings cause their own suffering may even explain much of what happens—but not everything.

• It may add to guilt rather than bringing forgiveness, healing, and comfort. Too often the wrong people hear a message like this. Those who already are convinced that they are guilty and all that has happened is their own fault will be crushed even more by this word. Those who are already suffering need to hear something else that will relieve their burden, not add to it. Often, the pastoral counselor finds that the biggest task is to help the sufferer abandon this view rather than to keep on applying it with a vengeance. It is difficult for people to discard because they know so many texts that seem to support it. That is why it is important for us to know about other texts that modify this idea, and to remember that it is important to fit the right text to the right situation.

● It may seem to paint a negative picture of a God who is preoccupied with looking for human sins so that he can find some reason to punish. Texts like these have led people to imagine that God is like a malevolent Santa Claus, who keeps a complete list of all our shortcomings, and who takes special delight when we give him some excuse to punish us. Many have stereotyped the Old Testament God as just such a Being, and have contrasted this picture with what they have seen in the New Testament.

This emphasis on the negative has resulted because of the many interpretations that have connected unpleasant events with God's punishment. We have pointed out (as in Deuteronomy 30:15-16, 19, and Ezekiel 18:30-32) that God does not desire the death or punishment of anyone. Far from it. His desire is that people will be obedient when they realize how much better it will be for them if they are.

The picture of God looks negative because people tend to raise the question about meanings when things go wrong, not when they are going well. In the midst of fame and fortune and happiness, we do not often stop and say, "Why is God doing this to me?" It is only when the bottom drops out that we ask this question. We think about God and interpret his activity when things go badly, and then he seems to us to be overly concerned with punishment.

● It is too presumptuous for human beings to know what God is up to in every single event. Maybe the Babylonians are being sent to punish Judah for years of unfaithfulness. But how much can a human being know about God's reasons for doing anything? How can we say that God causes everything that happens in this world? Did God cause the drunk to run over the teenager? To dare to say that God caused such a thing to happen and even to suggest some interpretation to support that statement is presumptuous. It leaves no room for mystery. It shows an insensitivity to others if we interpret their troubles as if we know something that only God knows. There is less danger if we make our own private interpretations of God's activity in our own lives—but to lay this on others is a very hazardous business.

● The idea of retribution works best when things are going well. It provides a way for the well-off to justify their status over against those who are not doing so well. It provides motivation for them to continue to live properly so that bad things do not happen to them. This view cannot help but drive a wedge between the person who prospers and the one who does not, the one who is well and the one who is ill. The spiritual counselor who approaches a sufferer with this view of righteous compensation has already said something about himself and the sufferer. He is not sick—therefore he must be a better person than the one who is sick. If God sends us what we deserve, then the healthy counselor must be better than the sick person. Certainly Job, as we shall see, felt this kind of chasm of self-righteousness separating him from those who came to him to explain what his suffering meant.

This view makes some sense for the objective, impartial, uninvolved analysis of how suffering fits into God's created world. It does not work very well for the person who is in the midst of suffering. It provides answers when the going is great and it provides cautions so that we avoid certain pitfalls, but it is small comfort for one immersed in pain, grief, and despair. The texts from this chapter provide material for the classroom, the sermon, and the Bible class. They are less likely to be appropriate in the hospital or the funeral chapel.

● This explanation of human suffering is too earthbound. As we have stated already, it expects God's justice within this life. That puts an impossible burden on this view because experience has demonstrated to all of us that it does not always work. The most common way of "Christianizing" these texts is simply to allow for a new, resurrected life in which God finally vindicates everyone and the seeming injustices of this world are swept away in the greater expanse of eternity. Most Christians have little hesitation accepting the principle of retribution as long as it doesn't have to work out within this world.

We shall get back to this again at a later time. As we have said, this view, as expressed in Old Testament material up through the beginning of the exile, suffers from incompleteness because it does not have the flexibility of allowing for a life after death. On the other hand, it makes it impossible to belittle human suffering as inconsequential, ephemeral, unreal, or a testing for future glories. These Old Testament texts do take suffering seriously and will not pretend that it is a matter to be dismissed lightly.

● With regard to Ezekiel's individualizing of this view of the cause of human suffering, there are special dangers. We are too inter-related with others, past and present, to be able to explain all our personal misfortune as if it was our own fault. Further, we cannot expect all bad things to go away if we suddenly repent and lead a new uplifting moral life. There is a cumulative effect to human relationships that cannot be swept aside as if events had never happened. We really cannot be children again and start over with a clean slate. (And even children do not start with a clean slate.)

If one attempts to apply Ezekiel's ideas without the advantage of a belief in appropriate compensation in *the next life,* the attempt is doomed to failure. Within this world, there are just too many pieces of evidence to overthrow this as a universal explanation for human suffering.

Further, Ezekiel confronts us with the peril of having to live the law perfectly in order to be rewarded. Everyone will have to answer for his or her own deeds. And it is not enough that your ancestors were good, or even that you were good for a time.

With Ezekiel, whether you live or die is completely dependent on your own ability to remain always obedient to God. Here you see the kind of dilemma that Paul got into. If you take Ezekiel 18 too seriously, if you generalize too much from what could be a helpful word in some situation, then you are doomed. In fact, we would all be doomed—because we cannot do well enough to deserve a good reward. To postpone our rewards or punishments to the next world only makes our condemnation more severe.

So we start with a basic biblical answer to the problem of human suffering. Human beings bring suffering and evil on themselves. God does not bring the evil, but his sense of justice requires him to set up sanctions. Things will go better for those who choose good than for those who choose evil. Suffering is, in effect, the result of human sin, and some biblical writers are not afraid to try to connect specific sins with specific sufferings.

This view worked for Israel for some time, even up to the point of explaining the great disaster of the exile. Not long into the exile, it becomes less helpful as a comforting word to those whose suffering seems overly prolonged and harsh and out of balance with what happens to other nations.

From the time of exile onward, this basic view is challenged, modified, extended, denied, but rarely completely abandoned by other biblical writers.

2

The
Power of
Negative Thinking

Is IT TRUE that a Christian is supposed to be happy all the time? Must a Christian suffer quietly and gracefully because of the promise of a better life to come? At least, that seems to be the message most of us have received. Maybe we read something in the Bible that convinced us of this. Or maybe we heard it in our own churches or from the smiling pious optimists on the TV screen. Is Christianity only for winners and not for losers? Where is one to go when the bottom drops out? What is one to say if the doctor has just hinted that you better enjoy this Christmas because it will probably be your last, or you have been told that your only child has drowned on a camping trip, or the pain killer which used to have minimal effect now doesn't seem to help at all? What is appropriate to say to God at a time like that? Should you thank him for being so nice to you? We Christians do have a problem knowing how to express negative feelings, or even knowing if it is legitimate for us to do so. We are surprised and fascinated by the character of Tevye in "Fiddler on the

Roof" because he dares to say things to God that we may have thought about but quickly suppressed.

In this chapter we will look at some of the least used, most lightly regarded material in the Bible—a section of Habakkuk, Jeremiah's confessions, and the lament psalms. These are passages about which we feel apologetic. We wish they were not in the Bible, we wonder why they are there, and we do our best to ignore them. If some enterprising young confirmation student or college sophomore looking for reasons to criticize his mother's religion stumbles across these texts, we are somewhat embarrassed and rather too quick to admit the limited usefulness of such material. An example of this attitude is the fact that lament psalms are by far the most common type of psalm in the Bible, but they are the least used in our public worship and, in fact, have either been left out or carefully edited in our hymnbooks to protect us from our own biblical heritage.

Something has happened to us so that we no longer know how to lament. A process that was natural and completely appropriate for an Old Testament person has become strange and even offensive to us. The first major section of this chapter will be a reflection on some reasons why we have turned away from these biblical resources for enduring evil and suffering. In the second section, we will look briefly at three examples of material dealing with the expression of negative feelings—Habakkuk 1:1-2:4; Jeremiah's confessions; and the lament psalms. The third section points out the continuing value of this material for the Christian.

A. Why Do We Avoid the Biblical Laments?

1. Overly pessimistic

We do not want to encourage negative thoughts and feelings. This material is too pessimistic. It promotes a neurotic preoccupation with self and focuses too much attention on everything bad. Would it not be preferable to divert the sufferer away from all the negatives and try to point out some good things that still are happening? "I complained because I had no shoes till I saw someone with no feet." "It's too bad about your son, but aren't you lucky that you still have two children?" "It could have been worse—you could have lost *both* kidneys."

Our overpowering instinct is to try somehow to cheer a person up, to get him or her to think about other things, to prevent too much dwelling on the unpleasant. Our desire to be of help will not let us allow too much lamenting. It is painful to hear. It does not make the sufferer feel better. For pastors, the problem is even more acute. They are supposed to have the right answers, the good word of healing and hope and reconciliation. Their whole function as pastor and communicator of the gospel is at stake. They ask, "How long can we let someone go on with such expressions of self-pity before we must step in and call a halt to the proceedings and pronounce the positive word which is ours to share?"

These biblical passages are too negative. A pastor with more than the usual training in counseling might let the negative expression go on for awhile, but sooner or later it has to stop. Certainly, you don't want to encourage its continuance by introducing passages like this to someone who is in the depths already.

2. Negative feelings toward others

This material expresses hatred of other human beings. Other people are blamed for most of the sufferer's problems and these other people are condemned in language that would be offensive to any sensitive person's ear.

You can only imagine what a person who already has paranoid leanings would think after reading passages like these: "Let those be put to shame who persecute me, but let me not be put to shame . . . bring upon them the day of evil; destroy them with double destruction!" (Jeremiah 17:18). "O God, break the teeth of their mouths; tear out the fangs of the young lions, O Lord! Let them vanish like water that runs away; like grass let them be trodden down and wither. Let them be like the snail which dissolves into

slime, the untimely birth that never sees the sun" (Psalm 58:6-8).
"Happy shall he be who takes your little ones and dashes them
against the rock" (Psalm 137:9).

These are rather severe statements about one's enemies, and the
kind of sentiment expressed here is not uncommon in cries directed toward God by the Old Testament sufferer. For someone
who has heard from childhood that a Christian is supposed to
turn the other cheek toward enemies, these words sound dis-
gusting and out of line with the teachings of the church. We
should not encourage their use. If people already feel like that,
then our job is to change their thinking, not support it.

3. Irrelevant for Christians

These Old Testament words are spoken by human beings who
lived long before the time of Jesus Christ. Therefore, it is common to dismiss them as irrelevant to the Christian message because they lack a knowledge of God which is now available after
the revelation through Jesus. This kind of argument is often
used to dismiss anything in the Old Testament which seems too
crude, too human, or in conflict with developing Christian doctrines.

Christians often act as if the second coming has already occurred, as if the realities of suffering and evil have already dis-
appeared, as if this world does not even matter because the next
one is so much better. In these and other ways, we have tended to
belittle the sufferers and their experience. We are telling them,
in ways more or less subtle, that their pain is not worthy of such
an overreaction. "Be thankful for Jesus who has saved you from
your sins and promised you eternal life. Praise God because you
know about Jesus, and don't dwell in the ruts of those Old Testament people who did not know what you know."

4. Too harsh toward God

We are unaccustomed to addressing God with the kind of direct assault often found in this material. We would never dream

of speaking to God like this: "Why is my pain unceasing, my wound incurable, refusing to be healed? Wilt thou (that is, God) be to me like a deceitful brook, like waters that fail?" (Jeremiah 15:18). "O Lord, how long shall I cry for help, and thou wilt not hear? Or cry to thee, 'Violence' and thou wilt not save . . . Thou who art of purer eyes than to behold evil and canst not look on wrong, why dost thou look on faithless men, and art silent when the wicked swallows up the man more righteous than he?" (Habakkuk 1:2, 13). "My God, my God, why hast thou forsaken me?" (Psalm 22:1). "Rouse thyself! Why sleepest thou, O Lord? Awake! Do not cast us off forever! Why dost thou hide thy face? Why dost thou forget our afflictions and oppression?" (Psalm 44:23-24).

Too often we pretty up our prayers, rather than let the words flow directly from our minds and hearts without first being censored. We must get our theology straight first, we must be sure that we have not left any gaping inconsistencies in our view of God, we must not divulge too much of our own pettiness and self-centeredness and lack of love—then, when we have done all of that, we shall attempt to pray. But to pray like these Old Testament people is not desirable. They talk to God as if he is responsible for evil and suffering, even though the dominant teaching is that we have brought trouble on ourselves. They address God as if he does not care about our suffering, as if he is delaying a response out of lack of compassion.

Sometimes they even talk to God as if they can bargain with him. They will try all kinds of devices to talk God into a positive response. They will appeal to his good name, his reputation among the nations, the promises that he has made in the past, even his vanity. ("If I die and go to Sheol, I will not be able to praise you because there is no praise of God by people who are dead. Therefore, if you want praise from me, you better keep me alive." This is implied in Psalm 6:5 and Psalm 88:9-12). Anything goes in an effort to convince God that he must do something to help in an otherwise hopeless situation.

This way of talking to God, assuming that we can persuade him and that he is susceptible to human arguments, is strange to us. To many, it seems to reveal an inadequate, primitive theology.

But is it really primitive or inadequate theology to believe in a God who is willing to hear me, who is influenced by my arguments, who is moved by my pain? Perhaps the really inadequate theology is the one that has God so boxed in by his unchangeableness and power and rigid execution of justice that there is no room for sympathy in his relationship with human beings. If a relationship is real, then God is open and vulnerable to being hurt, moved, and even changed by what his children say and do. There are many biblical passages (such as these we are looking at in this chapter) which show us this aspect of our relationship with God.

At any rate, one would not expect to construct a complete theology on the basis of texts like this in isolation from other texts. These passages do not attempt a systematic, rational, and completely consistent solution to the dilemma of human suffering. But, if it is true that the biblical material can be useful not simply as a source for the answers to our questions but as a resource for helping us endure, then we ought not be too hasty in abandoning what was so important in sustaining our ancestors in the faith.

5. The need for patience

Somewhere we have learned that suffering ought to be borne with patience and humble self-resignation. Until fairly recent times the traditional interpretation of Job emphasized his patience in the face of his many troubles, even though the attribute of patience would hardly describe Job adequately after the second chapter of the book bearing his name.

From wherever the idea comes, it is a common notion that we ought to bear our burdens gracefully; particularly this is true for men. Women are allowed a somewhat freer expression of emotion, though they, too, should not go as far as some of the psalms.

One could argue that this view is not biblical at all. It is certainly not the way an Old Testament person would think. There are some hints leading us toward a "grit your teeth and bear it" attitude in the New Testament epistles, but maybe it is something else in our western culture that has influenced us in this direction of a stoic, patient bearing of suffering.

Wherever it comes from, it is with us, and seems to be in contrast with the idea of lament, providing another reason for disparaging the value of a significant part of the Bible.

6. Self-righteousness

We are all sinners. There is no exception. But there is a strain of self-righteousness in the laments that is unacceptable to the person who has been weaned on Pauline Protestant theology. The problem with the world is human, and, though many Christians would be hesitant to see direct relationships between specific sins and specific sufferings, we are still convinced that the more general statement of the origin of evil is true. Suffering is a result of human sin, and everyone is a sinner. Therefore, in a sense, everyone deserves to suffer. It is only through God's grace that some of us do not have to suffer as much as we could expect and deserve.

Some laments have a confession of sins, in which the person who is afflicted admits personal responsibility for getting into such a state and asks for forgiveness along with action by God to remove the problem. Examples of this kind of lament can be found in Psalm 25:6-7, 11; Psalm 38:3-5, 18; Psalm 51:1-12; and Psalm 130. This willingness to take the blame for my trouble is completely acceptable. These psalms find their way into our hymnbooks and even become part of the church's weekly liturgy (Psalm 51, for example). They do not raise questions about God's justice, they put the blame back on ourselves where it belongs.

They are not audacious enough to claim that they do not deserve what is happening.

Most laments do *not* have a confession, however. It is not considered necessary to confess sins in order to lament. There are even a significant number of psalms in which the psalmist protests that he is innocent. Most Christians have been conditioned to look inward for the cause of trouble so that it has become unnatural to complain to God without also confessing our sins. We do not feel comfortable with bold assertions like these: "I have not lent, nor have I borrowed, yet all of them curse me. So let it be, O Lord, if I have not entreated thee for their good, if I have not pleaded with thee on behalf of the enemy in the time of trouble and in the time of distress!" (Jeremiah 15:10b-11). "All this has come upon us, though we have not forgotten thee, or been false to thy covenant" (Psalm 44:17). "Hear a just cause, O Lord; attend to my cry! Give ear to my prayer from lips free of deceit! From thee let my vindication come! Let thy eyes see the right!" (Psalm 17:1-2).

Again, we judge this material from our total theological perspective and find that it is inadequate in its expression of the doctrine of original sin. If you speak as these psalmists, as if you have been able to lead a perfect life so as not to deserve God's condemnation, then your problem is your own religious insensitivity, and the task for us, like Job's counselors, is to help you discover what a sinner you really are so that you can ask God for forgiveness and then he will give you relief.

Must we admit all our human frailities before God will hear our cry of anguish? The Old Testament laments say, "No." Our carefully designed theological doctrines tell us "Yes." What is one to do? How can our pain find expression in words if we do not honestly feel that we have brought our suffering upon ourselves? If the word of the lament is not available to us as a legitimate avenue of approach to God, we are, like Job, left alone and comfortless.

B. Analyzing the Biblical Laments

We have been referring to biblical passages that, for several reasons, are generally not considered very important and helpful for Christians. In this section, let us be a bit more specific and take a closer look at those parts of the Bible.

1. Habakkuk 1:1-2:4

Habakkuk is certainly not one of the better-known books in the Bible. Most of us would not know whether to spell it with one b and two ks or vice versa. And we would not know exactly where to find it except that it is somewhere near the end of the Old Testament along with books like Nahum, Obadiah, and Zephaniah. Habakkuk is most famous for the statement in 2:4 that "the righteous shall live by his faith." Whatever Habakkuk may have meant by this passage, it reached great heights through the teachings of Paul and Martin Luther.

Habakkuk is interesting for us because of what it contributes to our understanding of what the Bible says about human suffering. Most scholars would date this work to about 600 B.C., a time when Babylon has emerged as a power which cannot be stopped but before Judah has actually been destroyed. Habakkuk looks at the situation, realizes that the end of God's people is imminent and tries to understand why this is happening. He forms a transition between the answers provided by the pre-exilic prophet and the Deuteronomic historian and the answers we are looking at in this chapter and in following chapters of this book.

Habakkuk begins at the same point as the earlier prophets. He is willing to grant that God has sent the Babylonians as punishment for the sins of the people (1:12). This simple answer begins to lose its comforting effect, however, as Habakkuk sees what is about to happen. As bad as Judah has been, there is no way that she has been as bad as the Babylonians. Where then is the justice of God if the "punisher" is worse than the "punishee?"

(1:12ff.). The old understanding of God at work in the world to bring good or evil as we deserve it is being challenged in two directions—by the severity of the punishment upon Judah and by the lack of punishment on the oppressor (Babylon).

Habakkuk puts his question in a very audacious way, implying that God is not just, and virtually demanding that God provide him with an answer. "I will take my stand to watch, and station myself on the tower, and look forth to see what he will say to me" (Habakkuk 2:1a). In his approach to God, his raising of a complaint, his freedom to lay it all directly on God, Habakkuk belongs with the other passages we are studying in this chapter— Jeremiah's confessions and the lament psalms. In addition he is important because he illustrates what began to happen after the fall of Jerusalem—that is, the old interpretations of the meaning of suffering were challenged and modified. Again we see that the idea of retribution works better when things are going well than when the suffering actually begins.

Habakkuk gets his answer in 2:2-4, and here, also, Habakkuk is significant in giving us a glimpse of the ways in which the discussion of the meaning of suffering will go as the earlier view is no longer found to be sufficient. Essentially, the answer that Habakkuk receives is that he will simply have to wait. It will take time, but God's vindication will surely come. God is still in control. While you are waiting, trust him and stand firm in your faith.

This is a forerunner of a common biblical way of dealing with the problem of suffering—wait. Our horizon is limited—we cannot see what God is doing over the long haul. From here it looks bad, but if we could see far enough, it would be obvious what is going on. Eventually, the idea of waiting for the final working out of God's justice is put off to some future time or future world in the form of eschatology or apocalyptic. Habakkuk was probably hoping not to wait that long.

Habakkuk seems to be anticipating the kind of answer that is implied in the lament psalm and in the Book of Job. That is, the answer he receives is not a clear, intellectual answer at all. "Wait and trust"—those words imply a relational stance of trust and patience and would be less than satisfying to one who wanted some more tangible word of explanation. A common biblical theme is to give up on the search for intellectual answers and fall back in submission and trust on God, knowing that there is nowhere else to turn and that no completely satisfying answers to the perplexities of life are possible this side of the grave. Habakkuk seems already to be leading us in this direction. Whether he was indeed pacified by this limited word from God after the bold challenge to God in chapter one is not known. At least we have no record of his mounting the tower again and asking God to be more specific.

So, the little book of Habakkuk is significant for our questions about human suffering. It begins where the older view ends, and points in some new directions which will be explored in greater depth by later biblical writers.

2. Jeremiah's Confessions

a. What are they?

Jeremiah had been chosen by God for a special mission. But he complains bitterly about the price he has to pay in order to carry out that mission. In colorful and painful language, Jeremiah bares his soul before God and tells of his lonely and tormented life. He is sometimes so depressed that he wishes to die, he even wonders at times if God has betrayed him, and he seems to regard almost every other human being as an enemy.

Such material certainly tells us a lot about Jeremiah. The question remains whether or not it has an edifying effect on those of us who come after him and read these words in the Bible. There have been arguments whether or not these words could really have come from Jeremiah, but most scholars consider them original because disciples of a great hero of the faith would not likely ascribe such words to the master's lips if they were not authentic.

The following passages from the Book of Jeremiah record his confessions: Jeremiah 11:18—12:6; 15:10-21; 17:14-18; 18:18-23; 20:7-12; and 20:14-18.

b. Conclusions

● Jeremiah appears as a very human character. We know more about him as a human being than any other Old Testament figure (and probably any figure in the Bible). We know what made him tick and what made him hurt, and not just his actions and words.

● At times, Jeremiah is quite outspoken. The confessions are not carefully worded and balanced theological statements. Rather they are the outpouring of his pain and isolation. And so he is critical of God, hostile to enemies, and depressed to the point of death. He is not raising the question whether or not he ought to feel those feelings and think those thoughts. That is irrelevant. What is relevant is that those words express what was reality for Jeremiah, whether he liked it or not (and he certainly did not like it).

● We can put this kind of language down as unworthy of a religious person (as many do—and pity poor Jeremiah). Or, we can identify with it as legitimate expressions of real feelings.

● Jeremiah's suffering was compounded by the severity of the mission he accepted. Therefore, his case with God was different than would be the case for most of us. That is, his pain, in a very real sense, was brought on by the task God had given him. God had gotten him into this mess. And so he turned to God with his complaint.

● Through it all, God sustains Jeremiah, who remains obedient to the end. Jeremiah's talk may sound a bit strong at times, but he did not give up on God or on his task. And God did not reject Jeremiah for his lack of respect in addressing God Almighty. God sustains him, but he does not take away the job or the pain that goes with it. There is no happy ending. Although Jeremiah shows some glimmers of hope toward the end of his career, he never seems to become a happy man. For some reason, God chose this gloomy, cantankerous, hard to live with prophet to speak a word that we still remember and recognize as coming from God. All those smiling prophets of hope and good things to come are remembered only as a footnote, as the "false prophets" with whom Jeremiah had to contend.

3. Lament Psalms

a. What are they?

About one-third of the psalms in the Bible are laments. Further, there are characteristics of lament psalms intermingled within other psalms. And the mood of lament is found in many other places in the Old Testament—prophets like Habakkuk and Jeremiah, the Book of Job, the cries to God for help at the time of the exodus and the period of the judges, the book of Lamentations, the songs sung by David at the death of Jonathan, Abner, and Absalom. Lament is an integral part of the Old Testament. And yet, if one were to judge from the Christian use of these texts, this basic theme has been greatly suppressed.

Some lament psalms are for the community as a whole to voice its anguish over some catastrophic event, but the majority are for the use of the individual. Most scholars agree that both kinds of lament—community and individual—are intended for public worship. That is, the troubles, whether they be communal or individual, are to be shared in the presence of the entire congregation. One does not need to bear burdens alone, separated from a supporting community.

In recent years certain components have been identified as parts of the lament form. These components are the address, the complaint, petition, motivation (that is, why God should be moved to do something), vow to make an offering when relief has come, and assurance of being heard. Not all psalms will have all these parts and they will not always come in the same order. Nevertheless, there is a generally consistent flow within a lament psalm *from* an open pouring out of troubles to God *to* a positive statement at the end. The movement in the psalm is from the negative expression of despair to the optimism that relief is coming, from lament to praise.

Laments make use of powerful, symbolic language, particularly in the complaint. They use words that grip and involve a person at levels of emotion and consciousness far deeper than mere outward meanings. "Save me, O God! For the waters have come up to my neck. I sink in deep mire, where there is no foothold; I have come into deep waters, and the floods sweep over me" (Psalm 69:1-2). Such words, of course, are not to be taken literally (they are not applicable only to someone who is drowning), but they are powerful symbols that allow persons to say what they could never say in such an eloquent way by themselves. In the lament for public worship, one does not tell all the details of the specific hurt, but rather identifies with the common liturgical expression provided by the religious community.

b. The importance of the structure of the lament

The transition from lament to praise in these psalms is of utmost importance for our study of what the Bible says about human suffering. What happens in the process so that one who cries bitterly at the beginning of a psalm can be singing God's praises at the end? This is a key question for our use of these laments. If our goal is to help the sufferer, whether ourselves or someone else, to survive the ordeal and come out at the end still able to praise God, then we want very much to know what happens and how.

Some scholars talk about the change being an inward one on the part of the psalmist. A catharsis has taken place, almost as though the psalmist said, "I have had a chance to say my piece.

Someone was willing to hear me out and not put down my pettiness and pre-occupation with self and anger. I feel better now. I even recognize that some of the things I said were probably exaggerated and things aren't quite as bad as I have made them out to be. Now, if you have some word of encouragement for me, I may be able to hear it. I could not have heard it if you had forced it on me before I had time to get this off my chest."

Other scholars try to keep the interpretation of this transition from gloom to praise on a more objective level and have theorized the pronouncement of a word from God at the point of transition—after the complaints have been heard and before the psalmist begins to speak in a more upbeat manner. This may or may not be true. The evidence is not sufficient to be certain. At any rate, this view need not be in conflict with the former view. One interpretation tends to put the emphasis on the inner receptivity of the sufferer to be able to hear a positive word, and the other puts the emphasis on the positive word itself and theorizes about what person had the authority to speak such a word.

All of this has implications for us when we are called on to speak a consoling word. When do we speak such a word? What is the best time? When will it do the most good? When will the sufferer be able to hear it and not simply dismiss it as a lot of pious wordiness on the part of someone who "doesn't really know how I feel?"

Usually we say the positive word too soon. We do not have the patience, the trust, the willingness to go into the depths with someone in order to let the lament run its course. The psalm structures the positive response at a given point, though a specific individual may not be able to hear it at that point. A person will not automatically move from gloom to praise in the few minutes it takes to read the words of the psalm all the way through. It may take months of reading that psalm before a person is able to identify with all the verses and not only with the opening complaint. Nevertheless, the structure of the lament is a constant reminder that we never end with lament. There is always praise at the end. God has heard and has not forgotten and he will do something to get me out of this mess. The form of the lament tells me this, even when my inner feelings have not yet caught up with what is essentially a statement of faith.

C. The Value of the Biblical Laments

I think the biblical resources that allow the expression of a negative word are still valuable to us. In spite of the reasons for ignoring them, and sometimes as a challenge to those reasons, we would all benefit from another look at the use of the biblical material we have been discussing in this chapter. Let us be more specific in commenting on the value of these negative words.

1. Honesty

These biblical passages allow us to be ourselves and express the way we honestly feel. God means it when he says that he loves us as we are, even if we are in the depths, so affected by our agony that our thinking is not straight and our emotions are in chaos and any pretense at being other than a sinner is impossible to maintain. Even then God loves us. He accommodates himself to hear us from our own starting point. He does not argue with us, but listens to us. He knows how much we hurt, and he prefers honest words from us rather than carefully planned polite words that do not allow our true thoughts to be presented to him.

The laments are not meant to be examples to emulate. If one did not honestly identify with the lament, then one would not use it, and would be thankful that it was not necessary. We would not encourage anyone to feel bad, to indulge in self-pity. But, if persons are already at that point, then there is a word for them, also. The lament gives the sufferer words to use, a way of bringing into the open what is difficult to express, so that it may be acknowledged and worked through in some meaningful process.

No one wants to lament. No one desires to be depressed. If the depressed person could cheer up by some act of self-will, then he or she would surely do that. Any effort to bring consolation by urging a person to "think positive" is doomed to failure. Proverbs 25:20 puts it very well: "Singing to a person who is depressed is like taking off a person's clothes on a cold day or like rubbing salt in a wound" (GNB).

2. Evil and suffering

The enemies I curse may have truly caused me much suffering. The lament allows us to admit those facts of life. Too many of the traditional ways of dealing with suffering disparage its reality —even if in such a benign way as to promise relief in the next world. A meaningful religion must deal with life as it is, and life as it is contains too much evil and suffering. Lament passages are a logical consequence for anyone who has looked closely at the world. If one has never felt the need to lament, then that person is either lucky, isolated, or insensitive.

3. Trust in God

The laments actually show profound trust in God. It is easy to believe in God when things are going well, your life is filled with material and spiritual blessings, and you can approach him with a joyful heart and prayers of thanksgiving and praise. It is another thing to continue coming to him when the going gets rough, still trusting him to hear, confident that he can do something, knowing there is no one else to help. This is the point when those of lesser faith decide that their idea of God must have been a mistake and they give up the dialog, or they are so frightened of God's reaction that they never tell him what they really want to say.

It takes faith in God to keep talking to him and expecting a response. It takes a strong faith to be direct with God, knowing that he will not destroy you, but rather will hear you and help you. Even words of doubt expressed to God become statements of faith because they are addressed to the right person.

4. Relationship to others

The use of the laments puts the sufferer in good company. The walls of isolation are removed. A person discovers that other people have suffered in similar ways. Even the religious heroes of the past—Jeremiah, the psalmists, and others—had moments of great anguish. And they were pillars of the faith. If it was permissible for them to go through such experiences, then maybe I am not so bad after all, maybe my faith is not lost, maybe there is hope.

The lament puts the sufferer in relationship with all those sufferers who went before, and with all those who are alive today. He or she is given permission to admit how things really are and share them with others. It is one thing for the psychiatrist to say that it is all right for me to lament. It may be even more important for me to know that my religion allows me to do that. Knowledge of the presence of this kind of material in the Bible comes as a wonderful, freeing revelation to many people who had become convinced that good Christians should never feel the way they did. To lament at all is painful. To lament alone is agony.

5. Makes relief possible

The lament engages us in a process which, however painful, seems to be necessary in order to work our way through our personal suffering. We must go to the depths, face the pain honestly and openly, and then relief is possible. Attempts to gloss over the suffering, to hide it, to pretend it is not there, can only bring temporary relief and will probably cause more pain in the long run. These days we have evidence for this statement from a va-

riety of places—the steps in self awareness and rehabilitation of
an alcoholic, the grief process, the treatment of depression, and
the steps in the dying process. Not only those writing from a
specific religious orientation are coming to these conclusions. It
seems to be a fact of human life that true healing is not possible
until the full extent of the injury has been exposed. Healing cannot be pushed too soon—the complete painful process must be
endured. The depression must run its course, the alcoholic must
hit rockbottom, the grief-stricken person must admit that the
loved one is gone and will not return, the dying person must give
up the pretense that the pronouncement of death was all a bad
dream. Only when all is given up, when one has submitted to
death, then the power of Another can be felt and a word of consolation can be heard.

It is hard to walk with someone else through that kind of torment. If I am the sufferer, I have no choice. If I am the consoler,
my tendency is to avoid the pain. It is no wonder that we want
to shut off the lament and turn as quickly as possible to words
of hope and promise. It is not just to cheer up the sufferer—it is
also to save ourselves from the painful walk through the valley
of the shadow of death with another. To be able to go through
the depths with another human being—that is the supreme act
of compassion. That is more important than any particular, well
thought out, clearly articulated explanation for the origin of
evil and suffering. But it is so much harder to do.

The lament ends in praise. But you cannot short-cut the process. There is no easily-found happy ending. The agony will not
go away by leaping immediately to happy thoughts. The resurrection comes only after the crucifixion.

Laments and other expressions of negative feelings are gifts
from God to his church. They have been preserved for us by
our ancestors in the faith. As they sustained and comforted the
believers of old, they will do the same for us—if we can overcome centuries of disuse and recover their value for the church.

3

Suffering for Others

IN THE HOSPITAL where I served as chaplain, the young doctors who were seeking volunteers for the experimental treatment of terminal illnesses had an argument that was nearly irresistible—"Maybe it can help someone else." Those patients who were about to die were particularly vulnerable to that approach. They were struggling to find meaning in this unbelievable thing that was happening to them. And then the doctor provided at least some straw to grasp. Maybe it wasn't much—the chance to become a statistic in some researcher's notebook—but when you are desperate enough you will take what you can get. Maybe there would be some new cure so that future generations would not have to suffer and die from this disease. In some cases the argument would be strengthened because there might be a hereditary predisposition to the illness and the other people that you would be helping could even be your own children and grandchildren.

Recently the newspaper carried a story about a 29-year-old

racing driver who died of cancer. The story mentioned that during the last couple of weeks of his life, this man refused pain medicine because he knew time was limited and he wanted to be alert till the end because he was working to establish his own cancer treatment center. His suffering must be made to have some positive value for other human beings.

During war time, one hears many stories of heroism, in which a person gives his life for others—by distracting the enemy so that others may be saved, by falling on a grenade so that it does not blow up the whole platoon, by volunteering for missions where the chance for survival is slim.

An old grandmother has just lost a 20-year-old grandson to leukemia. She expresses over and over again the thought, "Why didn't God take me? I'm old. I've had my life. It will soon end anyway. If only I could have taken his place. If God had to take someone, why not me instead of this lovely young man with a great future in front of him?" Though she does not say it exactly that way, her feeling seems to be that there is a certain amount of suffering out there in the world that has to be distributed somehow. If one person is willing to take more than she deserves, then someone else will have less to bear. If we all deserve to be punished for less than perfect lives, then maybe my willingness to take on a little extra might make it better for someone else.

These are all examples of the idea that one person's suffering might help others and even save them from suffering they would otherwise have to endure. These anecdotes already illustrate two perspectives on this question. On the one hand, there is the person who is suffering and, in a frantic effort to find meaning, begins to wonder if there might be some unknown (or at least scarcely known) way in which the suffering could benefit others. If one can find even the hint of such a thing, it is a great help in surviving the ordeal. On the other hand, you have the example of someone who voluntarily takes on a mission that will benefit others. It takes courage to do such a thing, but at least the meaning is clear. The suffering does not come first and then has to be explained. Rather, the suffering comes later as a direct result of the acceptance of a heroic mission. In the latter case, the statement that my suffering will be of benefit to others is obviously true because it was for that purpose that I decided to submit to the experience of suffering.

Where in the Bible do these ideas about the value of suffering for others come from? Mostly they come from the New Testament, where the suffering of Jesus on the cross is such a central theme, and where the followers of Jesus are often exhorted to pick up their crosses and suffer for others as Jesus Christ suffered for them. (Examples could be multiplied, but one good one is in 1 Peter 2:19-25.) But the roots of this answer to the question of suffering are in the Old Testament. Later in this book we shall briefly look at how the New Testament brings together many of these Old Testament themes. But in this chapter, we will continue to concentrate on what the Old Testament says about suffering, proceeding roughly in chronological order, with special recognition of the historical situations which occasioned new modifications of those views that went before. In this chapter, the primary focus of our attention will be Isaiah 40-55.

A. Isaiah 40-55 and the Meaning of Suffering
1. The setting of Isaiah 40-55

For many years now there has been a debate going on about the dating of the part of Isaiah that begins with Chapter 40. Much has been written about that and this book cannot attempt to review the arguments on all sides. Nevertheless, the issue cannot be ignored completely because, as we have pointed out, God speaks a word to us in specific historical situations, and it is important to understand those original situations in order to make intelligent decisions about the application of a particular biblical passage to present situations. At the time of Isaiah 40-55, God's people had questions, needs, crises of faith that were addressed by this prophet sent to them by God.

Without a doubt, Isaiah 40-55 speaks to the people of Judah in exile. They have been in exile for some time, and there are new things happening on the world political scene which give signs of hope and the possibility of a new exodus back to their own land. Some students of the Bible still insist that all the words in the Book of Isaiah must have been written by Isaiah himself, and therefore Isaiah 40-55 would have to be written at least 150 years before the situation arose to which they were addressed. Whether that is likely or not, some people have their reasons for maintaining that point of view. What seems certain to me however, is that the words were meant to encourage those who had already been in exile for some time and to promise them relief.

After several generations in exile, there was discontent, disillusionment, and even disbelief among the followers of Yahweh. The old theology, as interpreted by historians and prophets, had explained the suffering of the nation of Judah as a result of the sins of the people. As we have already stated, this was the dominant theology up to the time of exile and continues to play an important role even up to our own time. But during the exile, there were some rumblings and grumblings. We have seen this already in Habakkuk and Jeremiah and in the lament psalms. The concept of retribution always seems less profound when one is suffering than it had seemed from a safer distance.

The following texts give a feeling for the atmosphere in which the prophet speaks his word: "Why do you say, O Jacob, and speak, O Israel, 'My way is hid from the Lord, and my right is disregarded by my God?' Have you not known? Have you not heard? The Lord is the everlasting God, the Creator of the ends of the earth. He does not faint or grow weary, his understanding is unsearchable" (Isaiah 40:27-28). "Come down and sit in the dust, O virgin daughter of Babylon. . . . Your nakedness shall be uncovered, and your shame shall be seen. I will take vengeance and I will spare no man" (Isaiah 47:1, 3). "But I said, 'I have labored in vain, I have spent my strength for nothing and vanity; yet surely my right is with the Lord, and my recompense with my God' " (Isaiah 49:4). "But Zion said, 'The Lord has forsaken me, my Lord has forgotten me.' Can a woman forget her sucking child that she should have no compassion on the son of her womb? Even these may forget, yet I will not forget you" (Isaiah 49:14-15).

The prophet's task was to try to rekindle morale. Surely some people had given up on God. After all, Babylon had won the war. What kind of God is it that cannot even win victory for his followers? The evidence would certainly make it difficult to support the notion that God was still watching out for his people. What had he done for them lately?

In that setting, the prophet speaks a word of hope and comfort. Their God is indeed *the* God, the *only* God. There are new things about to happen and the long-awaited deliverance is at hand. It has pained God to allow all these bad things to happen to the ones he loves. But now all that is over and God can hardly wait to get on with the return of his people to their homes. Suffering and oppression are about to end.

As part of his message of hope and comfort, the prophet has to deal with the question of the meaning of the suffering the exiles have endured.

2. Continuity with the past

With regard to the meaning of suffering, Isaiah 40-55 starts where earlier biblical writers left off. There is continuity. Older ideas are not abandoned completely. In short, Isaiah 40-55 accepts that a certain amount of suffering comes into our lives as deserved because of our sins. Israel had been blind and deaf to God's demands (42:18-22). "Who gave up Jacob to the spoiler and Israel to the robbers? Was it not the Lord, against whom we have sinned? . . . So he poured upon him the heat of his anger

and the might of battle" (42:24-25). God says, "But you have
burdened me with your sins, you have wearied me with your
iniquities" (43:24b). To Babylon, God says, "I was angry with
my people, I profaned my heritage; I gave them into your hand,
you showed them no mercy" (Isaiah 47:6). The people of God's
promise were told what would happen as a consequence of their
disobedience. If they had listened they could have prospered and
would not have had to go through the exile experience (Isaiah
48:17-19). "You were sold for your iniquities" (Isaiah 50:1), but
not irretrievably.

Texts like these that say that the Israelites deserved what they
got but now God has been moved to compassion are not uncommon elsewhere in the Old Testament. There are examples in the
stories of the exodus and of the period of the judges. The lament
psalms which contain a confession of sins are also similar. Up to
this point, Isaiah 40-55 has not offered much that is new in the
understanding of human suffering. The idea of retribution is simply accepted as the way things are. God is defended as one who
is just and has not caused suffering without some reason, and
the people who are grumbling about his lack of justice should
not be allowed off the hook completely. At least some of that
suffering of the exile was well deserved. But was all of it?

3. A new perspective on human suffering

Though the prophet is in continuity with the past, there is a
bold new step taken here. It is not enough to say that the pain
and suffering of the exile was a simple payment for past sins.
That is partially true, but it does not go far enough. Suffering
is not restricted to negative interpretations (as punishment); it
can have positive meanings. If we have the faith to see it, our
suffering may be part of God's work in the world to do some
greater good for other people.

This is an audacious statement. It flies in the face of past
theologies and present experience. It starts with an experience

which is almost universally considered to be negative and boldly claims that it is positive. The tone is set at the very beginning of Chapter 40: "Comfort, comfort my people, says your God. Speak tenderly to Jerusalem, and cry to her that her warfare is ended, that her iniquity is pardoned, that she has received from the Lord's hand double for all her sins" (Isaiah 40:1-2).

Double for all her sins. As mentioned above, she has been paying for her sins. That is part of the answer. But the real answer goes beyond that. There must be more going on than simple cause-and-effect punishment. The pain is too severe and God is too good for the older retribution concept to carry the whole weight of the interpretation of the suffering of Jerusalem. The people have suffered twice as much as they deserved. What, then, is the reason for the double dose? There must be a reason because God is loving and compassionate and it pains him to see us suffer and he would not ask this of us if there were not some reason. Isaiah 40-55 has an answer—a new element in our discussion of the meaning of suffering. Some suffering is for the benefit of other people. The suffering of a people or one individual can somehow (and the somehow is where the answer often becomes hazy and difficult to grasp) benefit other peoples and individuals.

There are several texts in Isaiah 40-55 which lead us in this direction. Israel is identified as God's witnesses (as in 43:9-10). In several places, Israel is called "a light to the nations" (as in 42:6 and 49:6). Israel, the Servant of Yahweh, has a mission to reach out to all of the world. The nations of the world will be moved by what God is doing through his chosen people and they will be persuaded to become worshipers of the one true God, the God of Israel.

The best texts for support of the idea that the suffering of the righteous may be of benefit to others are in the so-called Servant Songs. They are four poems that have been isolated from the rest of Isaiah 40-55 because of their special character. These passages are 42:1-4; 49:1-6; 50:4-9; and 52:13—53:12. There has been much

debate about these poems and there is still considerable disagree-
ment about them. We cannot enter very far into that debate here.
The most hotly discussed question has to do with the identity
of the Servant. The traditional Jewish interpretation is that the
Servant, even though he seems to be an individual, is really the
people of Israel. The question that is being raised, then, is the
meaning of the suffering of Israel. Others identify the Servant
in the poems as an individual—someone in Israel's past or present
(like a prophet who suffered because of his message) or someone
in the future. Christians can hardly read these passages without
thinking of their later embodiment in the life and death of Jesus
Christ.

We do not need to solve this question now (even if we could).
Certainly, Isaiah 40-55 is about the undeserved suffering of Israel.
But it is also about the suffering of individuals, particularly those
who are chosen by God for some act of self-giving and suffering
on behalf of other people. Whether we look on the suffering servant of Isaiah 40-55 as a single person or a remnant of God's
people or all of God's people, we still are left with the same
theological questions. How can one's suffering help another? Is
it possible to demonstrate how that works? Is it merely blowing
in the wind to proclaim that what appears as a negative experience of the triumph of evil and human agony is really doing
someone somewhere some good?

Isaiah 40-55 does make some efforts to explain what good has
come from Israel's experience in exile. For example, a large part
of the world that did not know about Israel's God, now knows
about him because the people scattered to all parts of the world
and took their worship with them. In a similar way, when the
early Christians were persecuted and scattered, their flight actually hurried the spreading of the faith. Further, the prophet
in Isaiah 40-55 tells how the nations will be moved by the way
the people have kept their faith and borne the suffering patiently
even though they were not deserving of all that was happening
to them. Since God was now restoring the fortunes of Israel, this

would be a sign to the nations that what had appeared as defeat and abandonment by God was actually the willingness to accept a very difficult mission. God's chosen ones are vindicated, and by their patience in adversity, many others will be won to faith in the one true God.

That is the kind of reasoning that we find in Isaiah 40-55 to support the statement that the suffering of God's people in exile was for the benefit of others.

4. The promise of hope

Even suffering for others has its limits, its promise of relief, its victory. There needs to be some vindication, a promise of deliverance at some point in the future, even if, as it becomes clearer in later biblical thought, that point may not come until the next life, the new age. God would not ask any human to take on suffering for others if there were not a promised end to it. The suffering is not an end in itself but makes sense only in the light of God's final vindication. God does not desire suffering for his loved ones. If they must suffer for the greater good of others whom God loves, they have the assurance that it will not go on indefinitely with no hope at all. The sufferer is not relegated forever to the scrap heap so that others may live.

The setting of Isaiah 40-55 is at a time of hope. The end of the suffering is in sight. It is in expectation of the favorable outcome that the prophet dares to put a positive interpretation on the suffering. Always in the Bible there is the promise of an end to the suffering—even if the suffering is for the good of someone else. God will vindicate the suffering servant (Isaiah 50:7-9; 53:10-12). Job will have his fortunes restored. The singer of the lament will be heard and relief will come. Jesus, dead and buried, will live again.

In the last chapter we learned that it was necessary to hear the negative before you can hear the positive. Now we are assured that there will be a positive. God does not leave us at the level of death and despair. Though we are not always ready to hear it, though the pain is still so intense that it blots out every other sound, though we may need to continue in lament for a time longer, the end of the matter is settled once and for all. The story always ends in hope.

B. The Meaning of Isaiah 40-55 for Today

In this chapter we have introduced a new wrinkle in the way the biblical writers seek to find meaning in their suffering. At this point, I shall make a few summary comments that will attempt to put this new idea in perspective with other biblical points of view and will speak to the question of contemporary pastoral application.

Again, we need to remind ourselves that there is no single biblical answer to the problem of human suffering. Just as it would be improper to interpret every single act of misfortune as a payment for some sin, so also it would be unwise to speculate that every disaster is really an example of God using my suffering for some great and noble purpose. One of the most common objections to this answer in specific cases is that it involves too drastic a means to achieve rather modest ends. For example, how could one interpret the slaughter of six million Jews as accomplishing anything worthwhile for the benefit of the human race? One could say that it stands as a warning against future tyrannies, or it helped motivate the western nations to allow Israel to become a political state again, or some other speculation would be possible. But any rationalization would be inadequate for an event of such gigantic evil. No answer can rescue an event of such horrible proportions and see any good in it.

1. The test of experience

Does this theory of the meaning of suffering presented so boldly in Isaiah 40-55 and picked up so enthusiastically by the

Christian church really work? Can it pass the test of human experience? Is it only wishful thinking, a desperate effort to make what is bad seem good, a way of talking oneself into a reason for carrying on in the midst of suffering.

Experience shows that sometimes it works and sometimes it doesn't. We can all cite examples of the positive value of suffering on the lives of people. And we can also think of cases where suffering has had a very negative effect. It is certainly not true that suffering, in and of itself, is a good thing. There is too much evidence that speaks against that easy and naive generalization.

On the positive side, one can think of examples where a family has been drawn together with new love and purpose by suffering that they have shared with each other. When one needs help at a time of suffering, it is best to look for someone who has been through his or her own moments of agony. The best counselors for those with alcohol or other drug problems are those who have been through that ordeal themselves. The best candidates for the ministry are those who have felt pain in their own lives and have known what it is to be comforted. It is difficult to walk with another through the valley of the shadow of death. But when I go through my own time of torment, I will look for a pastor who has been there and knows what it is like and will understand what I am going through.

We could think of many specific examples that show how one's own suffering can be put to the benefit of others. This is obvious with those who have chosen a particular mission of service that demands self-sacrifice, but it may also be true when we have not sought any such suffering at all. It may even be true in a kind of mystical sense which we Protestants do not understand very well. That is, there may be some way in which my willingness to bear more than my share of life's burdens may be of benefit to others. But this is so ephemeral, so spiritual, so lacking in concrete examples, that it is hard for most of us to appreciate. For those of a different piety, it may have profound significance.

On the negative side, we can think of examples where suffering in the life of a person has made life for others more miserable rather than having any positive results. More often than not suffering leads to disintegration rather than integration. When people get terribly ill and approach death, they usually get more unpleasant and make life more difficult for their loved ones. Most suffering and death is very messy. Many families suffer untold pain when the sweet old lady or lovely old man become foul-mouthed and nasty under the influence of biological deterioration. Many have thought that they have lost their faith at the time of the death of a loved one—particularly at the death of a child. Husbands and wives who have lost a young child are much more likely to split up than are families which have not gone through such painful experiences.

It is very difficult to apply this idea that suffering has a positive value for others in a general way. Sometimes it seems to work to the good. At least as often, if not more often, it does not. Experience would certainly challenge the wide application of this view.

2. The attitude of the sufferer

Maybe the important ingredient that makes suffering sometimes positive and sometimes negative is our attitude toward what is happening. Maybe we should say that suffering has only a "potential" value for others, and whether or not it ever becomes anything positive is determined by our attitude toward it. At the very best, suffering is neutral, certainly not positive in itself.

If one is open to God's leading, even in the worst of difficulties, then there is a chance that some good might come of it. We are reminded of the story of Joseph in Genesis 50:15-21. Joseph's brothers fear that he will now seek revenge on them for what they had done to him now that their father is dead and that restraint on Joseph's vengeance is gone. But Joseph is very forgiving. He grants that what they did to him by selling him into slavery was an evil act. It was not excusable. It had caused Joseph much suffering and separation from his home and loved ones. But Joseph was prepared to make the best of whatever situation he was in, and when it was all over, many people had been saved because Joseph was in the right place at the right time and had the wisdom to plan ahead for coming famines.

Joseph's suffering was real. The wrong that his brothers did was real. It is not even necessary to say that God worked it all out so that Joseph would be there in Egypt to help people. But, given the realities of the situation, Joseph's attitude of humility and willingness to be obedient to God turned his suffering into a blessing for many.

Our suffering has potential value. Whether or not we will be able to turn disaster into something of benefit to others may well depend on our own attitude. Again, if this is true, our answer becomes more of an inner relational one than an objective, intellectual one. If I am able to maintain the belief that God can be at work in me even in the midst of disaster, then something worthwhile may emerge even out of my suffering.

3. Taking risks

Suffering for others makes most sense when we have consciously volunteered for a mission, knowing the risks involved, but also being able to see the purpose for taking those risks. If one chooses to serve in the leper colony and then contracts leprosy, the suffering of that disease is understandable as a result of doing something for others. The suffering of Daniel in the lions' den or the early Christian martyrs at the hands of the Romans was a direct result of a courageous witness for God in demanding situations. This explanation of suffering for others fits exactly in that context.

But what about the run-of-the-mill, ordinary, unasked for, grubby suffering of common people? How can the suffering and death of a young husband and father be of benefit to anyone, least of all to his immediate family? One must stretch the imagination to believe that this can be true, and it would certainly not be an interpretation that an outsider would dare to impose on those who are closest to the pain of this experience. Maybe, some day, with the proper attitude and a refined faith, one of those involved might be able to give some assent to the idea that people have been helped in some way by his or her pain. Maybe, but maybe not.

4. Suffering that is sought

There is some danger that if this interpretation of the meaning of suffering is pushed too hard, it tends to glorify suffering as something positive, something even to be sought. Some people seem to think that the worse things get, the more they can be convinced that God is near. The implication would be that we should rejoice when things get worse, that we should seek suffering as a way of coming closer to God, and (worst of all) we should not work as hard as we can to remove the causes of suffering in the lives of people.

We do not want to give in to suffering too soon, treating it as if it were normal, or even desirable. It is particularly malicious if we teach such a point of view from our own positions of comfort and affluence. It begins to look suspiciously like a way of persuading the less fortunate to be content with what they have and not to be too restless in their aspirations for a better life.

Suffering may lead to some positive results. Particularly this is true if it comes as the result of a willingness to take on a difficult mission. But suffering is not what God wants for his people. The goal he has for us is the eventual removal of suffering and evil, not its continuance. When we suffer, it pains God as well. We hope for a time when pain and evil and death will be gone forever.

5. Suffering for others

Some of the Old Testament texts we have examined seem to speak against the idea that someone else can bear the results of our sins and get us off the hook so that we do not have to answer for our own deeds. Ezekiel, for example, would have difficulty comprehending these famous words from Isaiah 53:4-6: "Surely, he has borne our griefs and carried our sorrows; yet we esteemed him stricken, smitten by God, and afflicted. But he was wounded for our transgressions, he was bruised for our iniquities; upon him was the chastisement that made us whole, and with his stripes we are healed. All we like sheep have gone astray; we have turned every one to his own way; and the Lord has laid on him the iniquity of us all."

This passage certainly appears to be an alternative response to what Ezekiel said in Chapter 18, where he insisted that every person will be accountable for his or her own sins, that there is no penalty because your parents were bad, but neither is there any benefit because your parents were good. You stand there all by yourself. No one else can take on the punishment that is rightfully yours. Ezekiel was trying to defend individual responsibility, and if someone else can bear the burden that I deserve, even if that someone is willing to do it, it simply does not seem just. God's justice can be criticized from two directions—because he is too hard on those who seem innocent and also (as with Ezekiel in this case) if he appears to be too easy on the guilty.

Jeremiah, too, would have trouble with Isaiah 53, at least the way it has sometimes been interpreted. Jeremiah, himself, could almost be a model for the Suffering Servant in Isaiah. He certainly suffered on behalf of the people. If he had not agreed to be God's messenger to an unheeding audience, his suffering would have been much less. Nevertheless, Jeremiah would have difficulty believing that his suffering (or that of anyone like him) could benefit his people so that they would not have to answer for their sins. He was suffering because they did not hear his message, but they would have to answer to God for themselves regardless of what happened to Jeremiah.

The Jews continue to have a problem with the Christian doctrine of a vicarious atonement, in which the sins of all are somehow borne by one person. That remains one of the chief stumbling blocks between Christian and Jew.

6. The death of Jesus

When all is said and done, this explanation of human suffering for the benefit of others has its best application, and becomes broadly helpful to us Christians, only as it becomes part of the church's statement about Jesus Christ. We have tried to look at the Old Testament texts on their own terms, and we have seen that this answer to human suffering has some limited value for us at that level. But when these texts from Isaiah are considered in conjunction with the story of the crucifixion, then the answer becomes profoundly significant.

The process which Jesus' followers went through after the disaster of the death of Jesus must have been similar to the experience of Judah at the time of the exile. As it was not sufficient to think of the exile only as a punishment for sins, it was even less possible to think of the death of God's Messiah as a punishment for sins—at least not his own sins. There must be some other reasons why God let him die. The conviction grew that he had died for *our* sins, and Isaiah 53 was particularly helpful in providing words to articulate this idea. At some point in the church's developing theology, the death of Jesus became not simply an embarrassing event to explain but something that *had to happen*—a necessity—in order for us to be forgiven and freed from the penalty which our sins deserved (the retribution doctrine is still with us in one form or another). The resurrection showed that Jesus was indeed the one whom God had sent, and it indicates the final victory that will eventually come in its fullness. But the death was not just a passing incident on the way to the Easter glory.

The church maintained that something happened there that is necessary for our salvation. Christ died for our sins.

On this statement we Christians are all agreed—Christ died for us. His suffering and death was for our benefit. The question of "how he did it" continues to be more of a mystery. Various views have been put forward in the effort to explain in human terms how this could happen. Some of them are better than others. None of them is sufficient in itself. Some emphasize the outward, objective nature of the need for someone good enough to pay the price to implement God's compassion without compromising his justice. Other views put the emphasis on the inner effect this act of self-giving and suffering by God can have on the believer.

For a Christian then, suffering for others makes best sense in the light of the story of Jesus. Somehow, I know that I will be forgiven for my own sin and will not have to bear all the horrible consequences that would come my way if God's justice were carried out with unbending consistency. This removes the terror of judgment day. Also, Jesus' example inspires me to live a life open to service (even suffering) for others. Further, as I meet sufferings within this life, I can approach God with a confidence that he will hear and understand my pain because he has suffered and known pain as well. At least for a time, the suffering may not go away—but my cry of anguish will be heard and understood. As one looks for a human counselor who understands what it is to suffer, so we are blessed by our relationship with a God who knows what it is to suffer. As we cry out to God in the words of the lament, "My God, my God, why hast thou forsaken me?" we are profoundly comforted by the presence of one who also used those words in his moment of deepest torment.

4

God, Job,
and the Counselors

THERE IS ONE BOOK IN THE BIBLE which is devoted primarily to a discussion of human suffering. Job is one of the greatest writings in all of the world's literature on this subject. Other biblical books deal with the problem of meaning in suffering, but Job is the only one that probes the subject at such length and in such depth. Any study of what the Bible says about suffering must take a good look at the Book of Job.

Job is a complex book. Even after one has read it again and again and studied it in detail, it is difficult to know exactly what is Job's conclusion on the subject of suffering. On the one hand, Job has many answers to this question—all the best answers of the religion of his day are analyzed to see if they will fit Job and his situation. On the other hand, the conclusion of Job seems to be that there is no adequate explanation for human suffering. It is true that many answers are presented by Job's friends, but they are all rejected. And, in the end, God provides no answer at all—at least not an answer to the questions Job was asking.

There are two parts to this chapter. In part one, we will consider the answers to the problem of suffering as they are presented in the Book of Job. We will look at these answers in three groups, corresponding to three sections of the Book of Job—the prolog and epilog, the dialogs between Job and his counselors, and God's speeches to Job. In the second, shorter, part of this chapter, I will organize my comments and conclusions under two questions—"What is *the* message of Job?" and "What went wrong in the Job-counselor relationship?"

PART ONE: ANSWERS TO THE QUESTION OF HUMAN SUFFERING FROM THE BOOK OF JOB

Most scholars are agreed that the Book of Job did not emerge in its present form at the hands of only one author. There are differences of opinion, but it seems reasonable to suppose that there are at least three distinct stages in the development of the completed book. First, there was an ancient story about a man named Job, a righteous man who had a sudden disastrous turn in his fortunes. Since he had been a good man, his pain and suffering raise questions about the meaning of innocent suffering. Second, some unknown author at some uncertain time (between the sixth and fourth centuries B.C.) used this ancient story to frame an extended discussion of the problem of apparently undeserved suffering. The major part of Job is composed of conversations between Job and three counselors who come to comfort him. Finally, after Job receives no help from them, God himself responds to Job's situation. Third, at some later time, another editor inserted the speeches by Elihu (Chapters 32-37), a counselor who was not mentioned in the previous chapters. There is considerable debate about the value of the Elihu speeches but it is reasonably certain that they are an effort to update and improve the book of Job after earlier stages in its development.

The ancient story is told in the prolog and epilog. It is written in prose rather than poetry. This story tells about the righteous man Job and the calamities that befall him when he is caught in the middle between Satan and God. After a period of suffering, the epilog tells how Job is vindicated and his fortunes are restored. There are some interesting ideas in this material for understanding the origin of suffering. We shall look in some detail at them.

Then we shall briefly sample the answers provided by Job's counselors. We shall include the speeches of Elihu along with those of the other three—Eliphaz, Bildad, and Zophar. In the case of the latter three, we know that their answers are dismissed as insufficient by Job, and therefore by the writer of the book. It is less certain how we should evaluate the Elihu speeches because Job does not respond either to agree or disagree with the sentiments that are being expressed.

In our third sub-group we will look for the answers in the speeches of God, beginning with Chapter 38. These speeches seem to represent the culmination of the argument of the Book of Job (at least in its second stage), and therefore, they are the most likely place to look for *the* message of the Book of Job.

A. From the Prolog and Epilog

1. Innocent suffering

Not everything bad that happens to human beings is deserved. The law of retribution is challenged head-on. In fact, according to the prolog, Job is singled out because he is good, not because he is bad. God himself says that Job is "a blameless and upright man who fears God and turns away from evil" (Job 1:8). Many who have commented on the Book of Job have tried to turn this around and demonstrate that Job, by his lack of humility and impossible assertions of innocence, betrayed a self-righteousness that showed him as a sinner who really did deserve (or at least need) what he received. But that is not what is being said in the prolog. Job is innocent and does not deserve to suffer because of what he has done. There is no cause-and-effect relationship (at least not in all cases) between our sins and the suffering that comes to us.

This is a liberating word. The author of Isaiah 40-55 also pointed out that sometimes the innocent suffer, and, in fact, he tried to indicate the potential value of suffering for others. There is great comfort for a sufferer to know that all suffering is not payment for sin. The idea of retribution hangs on fiercely. We need help to overcome the tendency to turn in on ourselves whenever something goes wrong. Sometimes, it may really be our fault. But not all the time. There are occasions when we simply do not deserve what is happening to us, and it is comforting to say that clearly and forcefully and to know there are biblical passages that support that statement.

2. Satan

The Satan figure plays an important role in the prolog to the Book of Job. He is not present anywhere else in the book—in the conversations with any of the counselors, in God's speeches, or in the epilog. This is the first time we have encountered the existence of Satan as a way of understanding the presence of suffering and evil in the world. In fact, Satan is never mentioned in the Old Testament until after the time of the exile, in some of the later Old Testament books like Job, Zechariah, and 1 Chronicles 21. As we mentioned earlier, the snake in Genesis 3 is very much like Satan, but he is not actually called Satan in the story of the Fall.

In Job, Satan appears to be on good terms with God. It seems that he roams around the earth for a time and then reports back to God about some of the things he has seen. It is in the course of such a conversation that God brags about Job and Satan raises doubts about how long Job's faithfulness would last if things started to go bad for him. Satan is a tester, a character who seems to enjoy leaning on people to see how much they can take. Therefore, in the process of such testing, Satan can bring us pain and suffering. But he is not yet thought of as the source of evil, as the one who personifies the forces of darkness and cruelty and everything evil.

The Old Testament view is not a dualism, with a good God who brings us good and a bad God who brings us bad. There is only one God. In some ways it would help to explain at least some kinds of evil if we had an evil God to blame. The idea of a Satan allows us to move slightly in that direction, without sacrificing the sovereignty of the one God who has the final say. God does allow Satan to harm Job—that may be troublesome —but Satan has to get permission from God and there are limits set by God on just how far Satan is allowed to go.

From this time onward, the biblical explanations of evil and suffering will more and more make reference to some kind of hostile supernatural being—Satan, demons, the devil. We will see this particularly in apocalyptic literature and in much of the New Testament.

3. A test of loyalty

The prolog raises the possibility that Job is suffering because God needed to be convinced that Job loved him for himself and not because of the many blessings that he had bestowed. For those who become uneasy when the Bible talks about God in human, emotional images, this can be rather disturbing. God boasts about Job to Satan. By doing that, he allows himself to be talked into a test of loyalty in which Job has to pay the price for God's ego. The testing is to show whether a man like Job, who has everything, will still love God when he has nothing. Satan asks the question, "Why shouldn't he believe in you and be faithful? You have protected him and made him prosper. You know how human beings are. They are only interested in themselves and what they can get. He doesn't really love you.

He only loves what you can give him. Let me test him and then we'll see what really makes him tick."

And God is moved by that argument. How can he know if he is loved for himself alone unless he takes away some of those blessings from Job and puts him to the test? And for whose benefit is the testing? Is it for Job—so that he will have a more refined faith that is founded not on receiving good things but on a relationship that sustains and comforts and persists even in the darkest gloom? Or is it for the benefit of God—who can command all things, but who desires the love freely given by the humans he has created?

Do we love God only out of selfish motives? Do we serve him only for what we can get out of it—whether it be more of the treasures and pleasures of this life or the promise of an eternity of bliss? Is that what we want from him? Maybe suffering, not getting what you want, even losing what you have, is the one way to escape being caught in that kind of relationship with God.

These are interesting possibilities to ponder in our efforts to make some sense out of suffering. They are barely hinted in the prolog of Job, but some commentators have found them to be very significant.

4. A happy ending

In the epilog, Job has his fortunes restored and he lives happily ever after. What sense can we make of that ending in light of the rest of the Book of Job? On the surface it looks like a return to a simple-minded, naive belief in the doctrine that the good always get rewarded if they just wait long enough. The solution sounds too pat, too easy, after the struggle of the rest of the book. The problem is precisely that our problems do not always have a happy ending. In real life, Job would not get everything back double. For those who have been identifying with Job in his determination to deal honestly with the pains of the world, the epilog seems like a letdown. Some have even proposed that it must have been written by someone else because it lapses back into the earlier theologies (elsewhere condemned in Job) that tried to explain every success or failure as a result of good or bad behavior.

Maybe—but maybe not. Even those Old Testament passages that are most concerned not to withdraw from the reality of human suffering (like the lament psalms and the anguish of Job) want to show that suffering will end. The sufferer will be vindicated. Relief and deliverance will come. God will not leave us hopeless forever. There is always a good word at the end. It comes at the end of the lament psalm and it comes at the end of the Book of Job. God could not leave Job in that situation, especially since God himself had put him there for testing, not because of Job's deserving. The story would not be complete if there was not a word about God righting the wrong and taking away the suffering. There had to be a happy ending because God is like that and he has promises to fulfill. Since the Book of Job is not yet ready to talk about that kind of vindication in the next life, it has to talk about it in this life, and so we have the account of the restoration to Job of all that was taken away and the long and happy life that he continued to lead.

If Christians were telling the story of Job in a later time, they could have put off his vindication till the next life. For the author of Job, it still needed to happen in this life. So it seems a little artificial, too easy. But the need to say something about the final victory of God is there, as it is there in all our discussion of the problem of evil and suffering. This dilemma arises again and again. On the one hand, we want to deal honestly with the reality of suffering and not raise false hopes for the sufferer. Yet we also want to announce the final victory over that suffering. If the announcement of victory (the praise in the lament, the happy ending to Job, the vindication of the Suffering Servant, the resurrection after the crucifixion) comes too soon, before the depths are reached, it may seem to be false optimism. Again and again, the question for the one who would comfort the sufferer is to know when to say the word of hope and when to delay it because the lament has not run its course. The happy ending in Job is another example of this tension between the reality of present pain and hope for deliverance.

B. Answers Given by the Counselors

The major part of the Book of Job, from Chapter 4 to Chapter 37 consists of conversations between Job and his counselors. They had come to see him because they had heard of his misfortune and they wanted to help him, to provide some rational explanation for what was happening, to ease him through this difficult time and, perhaps, even to find some way to speed the arrival of relief.

In these chapters, then, we have a fascinating collection of what the pastoral counselors of the day were saying to those who were suffering. These were the best interpretations of suffering they had to offer. And many of these ideas have a familiar ring because they are, in fact, still widely used. They are still heard with great frequency in the funeral chapel or at the hospital bed. We need to remind ourselves that Job finds none of these answers helpful to him. Whether or not they can be useful in a different situation is another matter—but the intention of the Book of Job is to present all of these answers and then conclude that they are not appropriate to the case of Job, the innocent sufferer.

Let us look at a few of the answers provided by Job's friends.

1. The world makes sense

The old theology of retribution is upheld. There are cause-and-effect relationships between what we have done and what happens to us. "Think now, who that was innocent ever perished?

Or where were the upright cut off? As I have seen, those who plow iniquity and sow trouble reap the same" (Job 4:7-8).

The implication, of course, is that there must be some reason for Job's suffering. As upright, honest, and pious as he has been, there must be some defect somewhere that needs attention. If that could be found and corrected, relief would probably come soon. We know where the counselors learned this answer to the problem of suffering—from the same place that we learned it—the interpretations of calamity by historians and pre-exilic prophets. Perhaps Job's counselors were familiar with Ezekiel 18. Perhaps they knew of the curse in Deuteronomy 28:35—"The Lord will smite you on the knees and on the legs with grievous boils of which you cannot be healed, from the sole of your foot to the crown of your head."

From the prolog of Job we know that Job is not suffering because of his own misdeeds. His counselors, however, do not know that. They are still working with the older theology in a rigid and universal way, even though a close look at the kind of man Job was should have caused them some hesitation.

2. Sinners deserve punishment

All human beings are sinners and, therefore, are deserving of punishment. "Can mortal man be righteous before God? Can a man be pure before his Maker?" (Job 4:17). This is not yet a fully developed theory of original sin, but it does recognize that no one is perfect. The story of the Fall has shown that something has gone wrong, and the alienation from God that began then has affected us all. There is no such thing as a righteous person. Even the apparently "good" people like Job are really sinners and deserve whatever happens to them.

Again, we know where these ideas came from. We have already looked at biblical texts that support them. The trouble with this interpretation is its inability to make distinctions among human beings and it therefore becomes meaningless as an explanation for specific suffering. Even if you grant that all are sinners, then why are not all persons suffering the same way Job is? The question of why Job and not someone else still remains.

3. Life is tough

"I never promised you a rose garden." People who are as well-off and happy as Job was before the misfortunes accumulated are the exceptions. In the real world, the going is rough, and you ought not to be surprised when things go wrong occasionally (or often) because "man is born to trouble as the sparks fly upward" (Job 5:7).

There is a stoicism here—a willingness to put up with less than is desired, to lower one's expectations of what life ought to offer. Perhaps there is some value to this idea. Those of us who live in the twentieth century in the affluent west have become accustomed to certain optimistic views about the world and its progress and what we think should be a normal life-style. When we raise questions about the meaning of human suffering, it is on an altogether different level from the way the question would be raised in a third world country. We simply do not know how tough life really can be.

4. Be patient

Wait! From your limited observation, you may think that the world is unjust, that God has either lost control or he is not just. The wicked do appear to prosper. Those who seem to be innocent do suffer. But God will straighten it all out eventually. "Do you not know this from of old, since man was placed upon earth, that the exulting of the wicked is short, and the joy of the godless but for a monent?" (Job 20:4-5).

This is really an extension of the traditional view of retribution. We have seen such a plea for patience already in Habakkuk.

We will see it extended even further into the future in other biblical writings. Since it is often the case that the wicked never seem to get their comeuppance in this life, sometimes even living to ripe old age and enjoying themselves all the way to the grave, this answer works best when one believes in a life after this present one to correct the wrongs of this earthly existence.

5. Suffering is good for you

Yes, you may be right that you don't actually deserve it any more than, or even as much as, other people. But it is good for you to suffer. You should be honored that you are chosen, that God cares that much about you to keep an eye on you and discipline you and keep you on the straight and narrow and remind you what is really important in life. "Behold, happy is the man whom God reproves; therefore despise not the chastening of the Almighty" (Job 5:17).

The speeches of Elihu develop this theme at more length and in more detail than the speeches of the other three counselors. "Then he (God) declares to them their work and their transgressions, that they are behaving arrogantly. He opens their ears to instruction, and commands that they return from iniquity. If they hearken and serve him, they complete their days in prosperity, and their years in pleasantness. But if they do not hearken, they perish by the sword, and die without knowledge. . . . He delivers the afflicted by their affliction, and opens their ear by adversity" (Job 36:9-12, 15).

Suffering is good for you. It can bring you back when you may be heading into trouble. Though you suffer for a time now, you will be better off in the long run because you will learn things that will help you avoid even worse suffering in the future. Like small children, we need discipline to grow and improve.

This is an idea that has much appeal. It is a very common way of trying to explain suffering. Though still connected to a belief in retribution, it tries to go beyond the rigid view of suffering

as punishment and look for some positive value. It is not necessarily connected to the idea that my suffering is for the good of
others (as in Isaiah 40-55), but the two ideas often go together.

Elihu is not the first to expound this view (you can see it in
Deuteronomy 8:1-6, for example), but he does present it in a very
straightforward and significant way. There are students of the
Book of Job who like the direction in which this answer moves
and, therefore, they are also the ones who put a higher value on
the Elihu speeches (Chapters 32-37).

Job's response to all of this is a not too polite "No thanks." As
useful as all these answers may be in some situations, he is not
comforted at all by them. In fact, if anything, he feels worse, and
he certainly has become convinced that his counselors are against
him rather than for him. All of the answers mustered up by them
seem to be too pat, too intellectual, too remote from his own
reality of pain and suffering. He declares over and over again
that he is innocent and does not deserve what is happening to
him. He knows the theology of retribution, too. He had been
operating with the same assumptions as his counselors. But when
his world fell apart, the old answers no longer helped and his
friends were unable to find any useful new ones.

In his bitterness and frustration, Job lashes out at God and his
counselors. Job wonders why God is picking on him. In fact,
why would God pick on anyone? "If I sin, what do I do to thee,
thou watcher of men? Why hast thou made me thy mark? Why
have I become a burden to thee?" (Job 7:20). God has become
like a monkey on Job's back, watching him every minute, not
leaving him alone, preoccupied with locating sins that he can
punish. Job challenges God's justice. The wicked prosper and the
innocent suffer, and if God is not responsible, then who is?
(Job 9:22-24).

Job is also very hard on his counselors. He accuses them of
being against him from the start, as if he is on trial and they
are gathering evidence against him. He thinks that in the discussion of suffering they prejudice the case on God's behalf and

against Job—always assuming that the fault must be with Job and that God cannot be called into responsibility. He goes so far as to say that they are lying for God and that God will eventually punish them for that (see Job 13:1-13).

As the conversation continues, Job sees that his one hope is to have a confrontation with God himself. There is no place else to turn. The traditional answers of his friends are useless. They are so involved in their own answers and in defense of their positions that they lose their sympathy with Job and are not able to bring him any comfort at all. Even though Job has made some rash statements to God, he knows that if God will just hear him, just give him one little clue that he cares and that he is not punishing him for some unknown sins, that is still his best hope. But how do you command God to speak to you? How do you work up a religious experience so you know that you have been heard? That is what the sufferer really needs—even more than all the answers that the theologians have to offer. "Oh that I knew where I might find him, that I might come even to his seat! I would lay my case before him and fill my mouth with arguments. I would learn what he would answer me, and understand what he would say to me. Would he contend with me in the greatness of his power? No; he would give heed to me. There an upright man could reason with him, and I should be acquitted for ever by my judge" (Job 23:3-7).

C. The Word from God

From the second chapter of Job to the thirty-eighth there is no direct word from God. All the words are those of Job and his counselors as they test all the explanations for Job's misfortunes. But there is no word from God himself. The silence of God makes Job's torment all the worse, and he longs for God to speak, to give him some sort of answer, to give some meaning to his shattered life.

Finally, the word comes from God. It is not exactly what Job was hoping for, however, because God did not answer the questions that Job was asking. One is reminded of the response that Habakkuk received after his challenge to God.

The God speeches hold the key to the interpretation of Job. Everything leads up to this encounter. If we are looking for the central message of Job, then this seems to be the place to find it. But what are the answers? This much we can say:

1. The mysteries remain

Life and the world are full of mystery. Some things we can know, and we are to seek new knowledge. But there are some mysteries which will always remain. Job is presumptuous to raise the question of suffering the way he has. The best thing for a sufferer to do is to abandon the search for reasons why he or she is suffering and submit to God, admitting our human limitations and our pride, and trusting God to take care of those things only he can know and we cannot expect to know. This is not easy for us to do. We would like to know what God knows so that we do not have to resort to faith.

2. God cares

The response Job finally receives convinces him that God has heard, that he cares, that he has accepted his desperate cries for help, that he has forgiven his overstatements and exaggerations and delusions of grandeur. He knows that all those things said by his counselors do not matter. He can relax in his efforts to clear his good name. He does not have to wonder if God exists and despair because nothing makes sense. When God comes to you and speaks, the certainty of his presence swallows up the unanswered questions. Job probably can endure even if God chooses not to take the suffering away and restore his fortunes two-fold. All the other questions that had seemed so urgent and ultimately important fade into the background. The knowledge of God's love and concern has become the answer. "I had heard of thee by the hearing of the ear, but now my eye sees thee; therefore I despise myself, and repent in dust and ashes (Job 42:5-6).

When the events in your life do not make sense, when suffering seems to be way out of proportion to anything that you deserve, when none of the popular explanations for the presence of evil in the world seem to work, then it sometimes helps to contemplate the beauty and order of God's creation. How can you be anxious when you know that God is even keeping track of the gestation period of the mountain goat? How can you be anxious when you know that God cares even for the individual sparrow? God draws Job's attention to the marvels of nature. This is to impress on Job a feeling of humility at his inability to understand everything ("when I look at the stars I feel so small and insignificant"). But there may also be positive values for the sufferer in contemplating the wonders of creation when the world seems to be falling apart. As long as there is a rose, a rainbow, spring, a baby puppy, the ocean waves, the billowing clouds, there must be a God who made it all possible and who cares what happens to it. Many have found comfort in thoughts like these in times of suffering.

These, in brief summary, are answers to the meaning of human suffering as they are presented in the Book of Job. In the second part of this chapter we will summarize our conclusions by asking two questions—"What is the central message of the Book of Job?" and "What went wrong in the Job-counselor relationship?"

PART TWO: COMMENTS AND CONCLUSIONS

A. The Central Message of Job

There is so much here. It is difficult to sort it all out. Job provides many possible answers through the conversations with the counselors, the speeches of God, and even in the prolog and epilog. Of what value are they? Or is the only real answer the one where God tells Job to forget about finding any answer?

No one is an impartial observer when the question is raised about the meaning of human suffering. We all have our own histories and our own misfortunes. When we read Job, there are some words that leap out at us and say, "Yes, that is exactly the way it is. That describes what has happened to me and helps me give expression to my thoughts and feelings." Someone else, whose experience has been different, will be moved in a similar way by a passage which hardly seemed important to me at all.

As we read commentaries and other writings on the Book of Job, we are impressed by how much people reveal about themselves by the way they interpret Job—not only by their choice of which passages are the most important, but also by the way they apply those words to the experiences of life. There is, of course, a similar subjectivity involved in the interpretation of other parts of Scripture—but it seems particularly obvious with Job.

The structure of the Book of Job gives us a ranking of the various answers that are presented. We are not left to rely entirely on our personal preferences. The answers of the counselors are obviously not the central message of the book because they are rejected by Job. The answers of Elihu may be instructive, but they are not the primary message of the book because they seem to be a later insertion. So that leaves the prolog, God's speeches, and the epilog as the places to look for the central message of Job to the crisis of human suffering.

The rejected answers of the counselors are not entirely without value, even though they were not appropriate for Job. Most of them represent older biblical views as we have already noted. Though there is no single answer that ought to be applied universally, all of these answers could be helpful in certain situations. There is no doubt that they continue to be used by people who struggle with these questions. But counselors need to be careful not to force their own particular answers on others. That was what Job's counselors were doing to him, and he resented it. An explanation of suffering that is a genuine comfort to me may be a mindless platitude—or even an offense—to someone else.

The key to the message of the Book of Job has to be in the prolog-epilog or in the speeches of God. There is some problem harmonizing the prolog with the God speeches, though the editor of the book was certainly content to allow them all to appear together. The prolog offers some reasons for Job's suffering—the testing of his devotion to God, the insistence of Satan—whereas the God speeches do not offer any reasons at all.

This is not a conflict between different theories about the meaning of suffering. Rather, it indicates two different ways of dealing with the question. As we pointed out in the first chapter, the Bible deals with the question of the meaning of suffering on two levels—the intellectual level and the survival level. The former seeks reasons for human suffering. The latter seeks assurance from God of his presence and concern so that one can survive and not lose faith no matter what might happen. The answers of Job's counselors and the answers implied in the prolog-epilog belong to the intellectual level. The God speeches belong to the survival type. And, in the end, the message of the Book of Job is on the survival level. There is no intellectual explanation for our suffering. God will still be with us even in the depths, but we must not expect to have all our questions answered. There are things we cannot know. Live with that. Face it honestly. Have faith in God.

There it is. We may not be content with that. It would be nice to know why people, particularly good people, have to suffer. But we cannot know that. All we can do is trust God for what we do not know. It is *faith* that we are talking about, and not provable facts.

May we then conclude, with the last chapters of Job, that the answer to the problem of suffering is "to have faith"? If that statement is put before a sufferer as something that must be done, it can become a very frustrating answer. To tell people to have faith in order to bear their suffering is to tell them to do something that they cannot do. You can no more order someone to have faith in God than you can order them to stop being depressed or be six inches taller or change the color of their skin. Whether or not we ever have the kind of faith that is able to endure suffering is not something that we can will for ourselves. If it happens, as it finally did with Job, or as it is structured into the lament psalms, it is a gift from God himself. Though we cannot make it happen, we can at least be open to the process that gives it a better chance of happening. That means that, even in suffering, we continue to address our thoughts and feelings toward God (as Job did) and that we be as honest and direct as we can.

Is Job an anti-intellectual book? If we are told that the human intelligence can never find the answers to such persistent problems as human suffering, then how long should one stay at the task? Why keep looking for answers when there will never be any answers? Job, it appears, could be a source of comfort to the currents of anti-intellectualism that always lie close to the surface in the church. If the primary answer is to have faith, then perhaps it is better not to think too much. Why confuse people of simple piety with too many complicated ideas?

One does not stop asking questions because the final answer remains elusive. Even though one lives a life of faith, questions arise that demand attention. We are called to communicate our faith to others and to relate it to the real world. This means that, unless our faith remains an inarticulated mysticism, we must deal with some hard questions—such as, "Why does God allow human beings to suffer?" There are some answers to that question that are more satisfying than others. I need to have some working hypothesis, some tentative statement about the ambiguities of life in order to make sense out of the world. I may change some of my favorite theories about the origin of suffering from time to time as I grow older and my experience changes. I can do that because they are in fact only human formulations since I cannot know what God knows. *My* truth about the meaning of suffering is not ultimate truth—it is earthly, contextual, pragmatic, trying to bring comfort. If a specific explanation for suffering helps someone to endure that suffering, then it is certainly useful. If it does not help them, then it should be discarded. At the very least, we need to think about questions like this, with all the brainpower God has given us, in order to sort out those answers that are less helpful, or even harmful to a continuing faith.

B. Job's Problems with His Counselors

The Book of Job is important for our study of human suffering not only because of the ideas themselves but also because of the way the ideas are communicated from one person to another. A comforter may help or harm the sufferer in other ways than by the words that are spoken, as important as they are. Job reacted against his friends not only because of what they said to him but also because something had gone wrong in their relationship.

1. They meant well

The counselors did want to help Job. Do not be mistaken about that. They had the best of intentions. They were not cruel men who were blind to Job's pain. They were so moved by his situation that they wept when they saw him and they sat silently with him for one whole week. Some have remarked that that was the best pastoral counseling that they did. When they began to speak, they were much less helpful.

It is not enough to want to help someone who is suffering. The story of Job is a vivid illustration of that. Many who call on the sick and suffering and grieved find that they just do not know what to say and so they blurt out the most awful things. People who have suffered an illness or the death of a loved one have all kinds of horror stories to tell about how their counselors behaved. Their intentions were good, but that is not enough.

2. They believed in retribution

The basic point of view of Job's counselors was sure to cause trouble sooner or later. Though they tried various interpretations of suffering on Job, their basic stance was that human beings bring trouble upon themselves—and they were inclined to believe this even with regard to individual cases like Job's (as Ezekiel 18). So, even though Job looked like a good man, if you probe around long enough, there will surely be some sin that shows up and will explain why he is going through this ordeal. As Job continued to protest this line of reasoning, in more and more unpleasant language and with more and more exaggerated claims of innocence, the true nature of Job's sin began to emerge in the minds of the counselors. He was self-righteous. He needed to be brought down to size. Though he looked respectable, he was as big a sinner as anyone else, maybe even bigger because his sins were so subtle and difficult to find and acknowledge.

Job's counselors had a theory and they went in search of a sin. He knew that they regarded him as deserving of what was happening. And that put a gigantic gulf between him and them. If human beings suffer because of their sins, then the implication is that you (the sufferer) are a sinner and I (the counselor who am feeling quite well today, thank you) am all right with God. Now that is a real example of self-righteousness. And Job would have no part of it. The theory of retribution in the minds of the counselors doomed their relationship with any sufferer to failure.

3. They were too defensive

The counselors were defensive about everything. They were not willing to become vulnerable, to let go of their security and venture with Job into his valley of death and pain. Whenever Job complained about something they thought was sacred, their immediate reaction was to protect that something from poor, sick Job. So they defended God and their doctrine and themselves against Job's attack. It was like a knee-jerk response. They could not even hear Job say what he wanted to say. They were the protectors of God and the tradition. Most of all, they were protecting themselves from having to share the torment of Job. If they had listened to some of his objections to their answers, then they would have been forced to reopen painful questions which they thought had been satisfactorily answered.

Job knew what they were doing. They made him feel that they were his adversaries, that they had already decided that whatever was happening to him was his own fault and nothing he said would change their minds. In fact, the more he spoke, the more they were convinced.

Many sufferers have had experiences like Job when the pastor came to call. They have felt rebuffed and scolded when they have lashed out in anger against God or other people. They have felt that the pastor was less concerned with hearing and helping them than he was in defending a preconceived theological system that had no place for the experience they were having. Worst of all, they have felt that the pastor was defending God, always arguing in a way that did not allow for the hard questions to be asked, and, in effect, not allowing the sufferer to approach God directly. Rather than being helped to bring all their burdens to God himself, many sufferers have felt that their counselors have built a fortress around God so they could not get in. Many sufferers have never been shown the God who hears the cry of lament, who speaks to Job out of the whirlwind, who sends his son to sit with us on our own ash heaps of suffering.

Job's counselors were not able to show him that side of God. They were too defensive. No thanks to them, God broke through and approached Job directly. God's grace overcomes even our own efforts to restrict it.

5

Is There Any Hope?

DURING THE WORST DAYS of the Vietnam war, a small company of soldiers in an isolated area of the highlands met every Sunday afternoon for worship. The chaplain was finding it more and more difficult to know what to say to his men. Nothing seemed appropriate to their situation. What do you say to people who are risking their lives in a senseless war—a war that no one wants, in which you can't tell the good guys from the bad guys, and in which the people back home heap abuse instead of praise on their own fighting men? One day the chaplain happened onto the book of Ecclesiastes as he thumbed through the Bible looking for inspiration. That was it! "Vanity of vanities. All is vanity." Nothing makes sense. The world is crazy. All our striving is futile. There are no answers in this world. He was not able to preach with the usual Christian optimism—not right now. He still hoped everything would come out all right in the end, but in Vietnam in those days that hope was so far off that all he could do was agree that life was meaningless. So the next sermon was from this strange book that leans toward cynicism. It was so well received that the men would not let him preach from any other biblical book for the next five Sundays. Someone had finally spoken to them where they were, not where they were expected to be.

Life was hard for black slaves in Mississippi in the early nineteenth century. They were religious people, learning the faith of their masters, and learning it well. They longed for an end to the sufferings of this life. But they knew that they could never hope for anything better. And so they dreamed about the joys of the next life, when suffering would be gone forever and there would be no more hard work, no more stifling heat, and no cruel taskmaster (he would be punished for the way he had treated them). They were nourished and comforted by texts like: ". . . and they shall beat their swords into plowshares, and their spears into pruning hooks; nation shall not lift up sword against nation, neither shall they learn war any more; but they shall sit every man under his vine and under his fig tree, and none shall make them afraid; for the mouth of the Lord of hosts has spoken" (Micah 4:3b-4). They dreamed about what the new life would be like and sang songs that described it in great detail. Though there was nothing they could do to improve their present status, they knew that the pains of this world would not last long and would be insignificant in comparison with what was to come. By putting up with their present suffering and remaining obedient to God's will, they knew that the rewards of eternal bliss would be theirs.

In the late 1960s, churches in middle class suburbs suddenly became interested in biblical texts which talk about the end of the world. Books like Daniel and Revelation and Ezekiel 38-39 were studied and analyzed as if they were the most important books in the Bible. Small groups were formed to devote themselves to a thorough study of the Bible in order to find clues about when and how the world will come to an end. They were convinced that this would happen soon. They looked forward to it, they took delight in thinking about it, they enjoyed sharing new interpretations of cryptic biblical prophecies with each other, and, above all, they planned to be ready when the final trumpet sounds. Unlike the black slaves in Mississippi, this strange phenomenon was taking place among some of the world's most affluent and privileged people—ones who, on the surface, would seem to be having such a good life that they would hardly be in a hurry to have it end.

The people in these stories share the conviction that the world does not make sense. They cannot see any pattern or order. Rewards and punishments do not come to those who deserve them. There seem to be no discernible connections between what people do and what happens to them. The texts which these people chose —Ecclesiastes, Micah 4:3-4, Daniel, Revelation, and Ezekiel 38-39—provided them with support as they tried to deal with the lack of meaning in this life.

Ecclesiastes sums it up—all is vanity. He has no hope that things are going to get better in the future, that the injustices of today will be remedied, or that the present patterns of life and death will change. This world is all that there is. There is no future life for the individual or a future age for the world as a whole. Therefore, the author of Ecclesiastes proposes to make the best possible use of the present. As imperfect and meaningless as it is, it is still all that we have.

The other biblical writers referred to above see little meaning in the present world either—God's justice is not working out. Good people are suffering and evil is everywhere. But, unlike Ecclesiastes, they do believe that better things are coming. Therefore, the present world is negated, having little or no value, and our attention is drawn almost completely toward the future.

The world makes no sense—at least according to our expectations for the way things ought to be. Ecclesiastes suggests that we enjoy the present because that is all we will ever have. The other writers tell us not to mind the pains of the present because they will be completely swept away in the glories of the new age. Ecclesiastes gives us a present with no future. The others give us a future with no present.

These two radically different conclusions are probably due to the contrast in the settings of these biblical writings. The writer of Ecclesiastes has a present that is apparently not so unpleasant. His suffering is not an obvious pain or deprivation or oppression. But he knows that the good things in life cannot last. His suffering is influenced by his keen insight about the insecurity of life and its pleasures and accomplishments. He can tell us to enjoy the present because for him it is better than the oblivion that he sees in the future.

For the authors of these texts from Micah, Daniel, Ezekiel and Revelation, there is little in the present world that is pleasant enough to worry about losing. Rather, the sooner the present order of things ends and a new order emerges the better it will be. The present is so full of suffering and evil that it has no meaning other than as a stage in the transition from this existence to a future and better one.

This is our last chapter on what the Old Testament says about the meaning of suffering. We have traveled a good distance from the self-confidence of the historian (as in 2 Kings 17) or the prophet (as in Ezekiel 18), who are able to look at the sufferings of nations and individuals and find some cause in the sinful behavior of the sufferer. That basic view has been challenged by Job, expanded by Isaiah 40-55 and Elihu, and ignored by God's speeches at the end of Job.

In this chapter we will look at passages that support the view that, as far as this world is concerned, we cannot make any sense out of suffering. The concept of retribution does not work at all for Ecclesiastes. For the author of Revelation it still works—but not in this life, only in the next one.

Let us look at these texts in more detail.

A. Ecclesiastes

Ecclesiastes was written by an unknown sage, probably in the third century B.C. The author (let us call him the Preacher) seems to have been a person of intelligence, affluence, and importance. He had experienced most of the best things of life and still found them lacking in permanent significance. Many commentators have seen some Greek influence on this book. Ecclesiastes 12:9-14 is apparently an editorial postscript and helps to restore some orthodox credibility to the book. That and its association with Solomon probably influenced the inclusion of the book in the Bible even though it seems out of harmony with many biblical themes.

1. The message of Ecclesiastes

● "All is vanity." The book begins and ends with this conclusion (1:2 and 12:8). Nothing in this world is permanent. All our ideals, hard work, enjoyments of the senses, and intellectual accomplishments are only temporary and fleeting. Everything human will soon pass away, including our answers to the most troublesome religious questions.

"Then I saw all the work of God, that man cannot find out the work that is done under the sun. However much man may toil in seeking, he will not find it out; even though a wise man claims to know, he cannot find it out" (Ecclesiastes 8:17).

● Death is the great equalizer. This is the root of the problem for the Preacher. This world makes no sense and yet this world is all there is. Death washes away all human accomplishment. What is the point of working hard, achieving much, living the ethical life, if the good that we do dies with us? One fate awaits us all—the fool and the wise man (2:14-16), humans and beasts

(3:19-20)—we all return to the dust from which we came. When I die I must leave all the fruits of my toil to someone else, and whether he is wise or a fool, I can do nothing about it. He is now master of all the things for which I devoted my life and labor (2:18-19).

Death is the end of all things. Even if I have a good life (as the Preacher evidently did), that is not enough. Death is the final tragedy that confronts everyone, and, in a sense, the pain of that insight may be even greater for the wise man who sees clearly what death means and who has the most to lose. "But he who is joined with all the living has hope, for a living dog is better than a dead lion. For the living know that they will die, but the dead know nothing, and they have no more reward, but the memory of them is lost" (9:4-5).

● The world abounds with examples of injustice. The good life does not necessarily come to the good people nor are wicked people always called into account for their behavior. So the Preacher is caught in between—he denies the older view of retribution but does not yet believe in an afterlife which can set things straight. He is too wise to say that justice will come within this life—his experience denies that. To have that kind of honesty about this world without the hope of a new world puts the Preacher in a very painful position.

"There is a vanity which takes place on earth, that there are righteous men to whom it happens according to the deeds of the wicked, and there are wicked men to whom it happens according to the deeds of the righteous" (8:14). All is vanity "since one fate comes to all, to the righteous and the wicked, to the good and the evil, to the clean and the unclean, to him who sacrifices and him who does not sacrifice. As is the good man, so is the sinner . . ." (9:2). "Again I saw that under the sun the race is not to the swift, nor the battle to the strong, nor bread to the wise, nor riches to the intelligent, nor favor to the men of skill; but time and chance happen to them all" (9:11).

• In such a world, and with such a hope for the future, the Preacher can do little more than to affirm the good things of this life and to encourage persons to enjoy what they have to its fullest because the time is coming all too soon when all will be gone. Eat and drink with enjoyment. Do not shun whatever luxuries are available to you. Enjoy your work which you have been given in your station in life. Find pleasure in the relationship with your wife whom you love. Live more intensely now— this is all there is so don't waste it. (Examples of these thoughts in 2:24-25; 3:12-13; 3:22; 5:18-20; 8:15.) "Whatever your hand finds to do, do it with your might; for there is no work or thought or knowledge or wisdom in Sheol, to which you are going" (9:10).

2. The value of Ecclesiastes

It is not surprising that Ecclesiastes causes some raised eyebrows among Christians. If a belief in life after death is at the center of the Christian message, then what is the place of a book which does not know that hope? More specifically, what value is there here for the understanding of human suffering and/or the consolation of the sufferer?

• Ecclesiastes, like the lament psalm and the confessions of Jeremiah and the outbursts of Job, allows the expression of the negative. There is nothing frivolous or uninformed about the Preacher's position. He has looked at the world. He knows what he is talking about. He is painfully honest in his denial of the solutions of the wise to the great questions of human suffering. He will not accept what he cannot verify in the experience of the world—and he has the courage to say so.

There can be positive value in the expression of the negative— if it in fact represents the way we think and feel. God meets us even at these low points and it is for our benefit that the Bible has left us some of these negative expressions as a way of helping us present our thoughts before God. Ecclesiastes, strangely, still believed in God and found some comfort in that, even though his doubts were more persistent and he was less easily gratified than most other biblical writers. Like the Preacher, it is better for us, when greatly troubled, to continue to bring our questions before God and not drift away into disbelief.

● The Preacher's emphasis on the present is not without some value. Do not live only for the future, always hoping for something better, never able to make the most of what life has already given you. Live life to its fullest as a precious gift from God.

If the weakness of the Old Testament is that it is too bogged down in the things of this world (human suffering, events in history, the land of Israel, people and politics), then we could also say that a danger for Christianity is that it becomes so concerned with the next world that it does not take the present world seriously enough. We shall speak of this again under the section on apocalyptic. At any rate, Ecclesiastes, by its refusal to see anything other than this world, is a constant reminder not to live as if this world did not matter.

● Ecclesiastes is particularly a word to the well-off, successful, even affluent, for whom the present life is seldom marked by suffering. It is a message that many identify with because, like the Preacher, they have not been denied many of the luxuries of life, but their suffering is of a different order. They suffer because they know that patterns of reward and punishment in this life do not always work—and they know this even though they might be tempted to look on their own good fortune as a result of their good character. Though they "have it made," they are sensitive enough to be moved by the sufferings of others, whether earned or unearned. Further, they suffer, like the Preacher, because they know that it will all end in death, the great equalizer, the final statement on all human presumptions.

The words of Ecclesiastes strike a responsive chord in an age of disillusionment, when old certainties are lost, when trusted institutions fail us, when wars are no longer clearly fought between the good and the bad. So Ecclesiastes speaks well to our day, to those who seem to have everything but fail to see permanent meanings, who are moved by pain and suffering among others, who fear their own death, and who want to affirm the values of this life but are having a hard time doing so.

Ecclesiastes is not at the heart of the Christian message. But it is there if we need it. If the present condition of our life needs words like this to give our faith expression, to continue the dialog with God, to know that we are not alone in our search for meaning, then it is good that Ecclesiastes is in our Bible.

B. Prophetic Eschatology

There are several places in the prophetic books where eschatology—expectation about the end of the world—is expressed in words of great beauty. The prophets often spoke words of doom, and we have looked at some of those words because they have conditioned our tendencies toward acceptance of the retribution doctrine. But prophets also promised hope, deliverance, and new beginnings. The message of doom was important as a warning before disaster struck. The words of hope were more appropriate after calamities had already occurred and the people needed to be convinced that this was not the end of the story. Some of these words of hope may have originated later than the rest of the books in which they are contained (e.g., most believe that Amos would not have said the words in Amos 9:11-15), but they were included by later editors in order to bring the message up to date and make it more complete.

Some examples of passages to be included in this category are Micah 4:1-4 (with parallel passage in Isaiah 2:2-4), Isaiah 11:1-9, Jeremiah 31:31-34, Amos 9:11-15, Micah 5:2-4, and Jeremiah 33:14-18.

1. The promise of eschatology

These passages put an open end on the older belief that people eventually will receive what they deserve. The time for the fulfillment of those promises is put off into the future and is presented in beautiful, poetic language. Prophetic eschatology expresses a profound longing for a time when suffering will end, peace and order will be the natural way of life for all of God's creatures, and all human needs will be provided. Hostility and depression and guilt and oppression will be gone forever. People will finally know in their hearts how to live at peace with one another.

"And they shall beat their swords into plowshares, and their spears into pruning hooks; nation shall not lift up sword against nation, neither shall they learn war any more" (Isaiah 2:4).

"The wolf shall dwell with the lamb, and the leopard shall lie down with the kid, and the calf and the lion and the fatling together, and a little child shall lead them. The cow and the bear shall feed; their young shall lie down together; and the lion shall eat straw like an ox. The sucking child shall play over the hole of the asp, and the weaned child shall put his hand on the adder's den. They shall not hurt or destroy in all my holy mountain: for the earth shall be full of the knowledge of the Lord as the waters cover the sea" (Isaiah 11:6-9).

"Behold the days are coming, says the Lord, when the plow-man shall overtake the reaper and the treader of grapes him who sows the seed; the mountains shall drip sweet wine, and all the hills shall flow with it" (Amos 9:13).

"Behold the days are coming, says the Lord, when I will make a new covenant with the house of Israel and the house of Judah. ... I will put my law within them, and I will write it upon their hearts; and I will be their God, and they shall be my people" (Jeremiah 31:31, 33b).

Sometimes the prophets seem to be hoping for a rejuvena-tion of the world as it had been known, as if there is still some hope if the people return from exile and rebuild their cities and regain their political freedom. At other times, their hopes are expressed in such exalted language that they seem to be hoping for a new existence which is so different from the world that we live in that it has to be spoken of as a new age. Sometimes the prophets appear to be still hoping that *this* world will be renewed. At other times, their hope is for a completely *new* world.

When the prophets talk of an existence where there is no war, where wild and domestic animals sleep together in peace, where the fields and vineyards bountifully supply everyone's needs, and where all people know what God's will is and actually do it— they certainly seem to be longing for a world that has not yet occurred and can hardly occur this side of the grave or the Second Coming. The beauty and loftiness of this language can be used by those coming later to comfort them in their distress as they make their way through present sufferings to better times off in the future—whether later in this life or, more likely, in the next one.

Some of the prophets, though not all of them, expressed their hope for the future in terms of new leadership God would raise up to usher in new golden days of peace, prosperity, and joy. The leader would be a descendant of David, the greatest king of the past. The best examples of these texts are Isaiah 7:14, Isaiah 9:6-7, Isaiah 11:1-5, Micah 5:2-4, and Jeremiah 33:14-18. These texts which hope for a new messiah (the "anointed" king) have become of great importance to Christians who have used them to help explain who Jesus was and what part he played in the fulfillment of these prophetic hopes.

In these examples of prophetic eschatology, the prophet is not promising a personal resurrection and the possibility of an eternal life. We can read that into these words from our later perspective, but the words do not explicitly make that promise. There is no question that a better life is promised for God's people, but that does not mean that all people presently living will be alive to participate as individuals in that new age. There is still a sense of community in these Old Testament passages that keeps them from being preoccupied with concern for *individual* existence into eternity. It seems to be enough, at least for some, to know that God is still at work in the world, that his covenant with his people will be renewed, and the life of the individual continues as part of that ongoing relationship between God and his children.

2. The value of prophetic eschatology

It provides words for expressing our hope for eventual deliverance from suffering and misery. God will not let the present state of affairs go on forever. Over and over we have seen this promise presented to God's people as they come to him with their cries of pain. "Wait. Better times are coming. I have not abandoned you." This is the answer given to Habakkuk and to the psalmist and to Job. In this beautiful language of the prophetic hope, we are able to put the answer further off into the future. The sense of urgency and need for immediate vindication is relieved.

In our distress we find it easy to identify with the words of longing for peace and plenty and rest and joy provided by the prophets. They become our own words as we use them and fit them to our own private yearnings. There is no question that much comfort has been given by the sharing of passages such as these.

With regard to our search for the biblical answers to the question of "why" there is suffering, prophetic eschatology does not really provide much that is new except, perhaps, to open up the future somewhat and give us a little more time. It does not propose bold new intellectual answers to the questions of why the faithful suffer, but, rather, supports them in the midst of their suffering. "Continue to trust in God who will not allow the present suffering to continue forever. Though you still may not know why you are suffering, you can be assured that the final outcome of things is in God's hands."

C. Apocalyptic

1. What is apocalyptic literature?

a. Characteristics of apocalyptic

There has been considerable debate about the definition of what apocalyptic is and what it is not. For our purposes, I will short-cut that discussion and suggest that apocalyptic has at least these characteristics:

● Life is a war between good and evil and history will one day come to an end in a battle between God and all the forces of evil. God, of course, will win.

● What is happening in the world now can be interpreted as part of the scenario leading up to that final battle. For those who have the insight, the ability to see the signs, it should be evident that the final time is drawing very near.

● Apocalyptic literature uses a code language to talk about what is happening. Stories are told of strange beasts and other creatures that are symbols usually for certain kingdoms or persons. The cryptic nature of the writing makes it easy to misinterpret. Every age, it seems, is inclined to identify the beasts with persons and events in its own time.

● After the great battle in which evil is defeated, there will be a new age in which the oppressed will be vindicated and oppressors will be punished.

● People will be brought back to life so they can receive the proper reward or punishment they may have missed in this life. This is important because the world does not make sense without this possibility. Martyrs must be given a new opportunity for life in order to justify the laying down of their lives for a cause. Tyrants who have caused the faithful much suffering will have to be brought to justice, even if they have died in a pleasant old age. Therefore, a resurrection is necessary in order to put all things in good order.

b. Old Testament examples of apocalyptic

The best example of apocalyptic in the Old Testament is probably the Book of Daniel. This book presents the clearest statement of a belief in resurrection in the Old Testament:

> At that time shall arise Michael, the great prince who has charge of your people. And there shall be a time of trouble, such as never has been since there was a nation till that time; but at that time your people shall be delivered, every one whose name shall be found written in the book. And many of those who sleep in the dust of the earth shall awake, some to everlasting life, and some to shame and everlasting contempt (Daniel 12:1-2).

Another example is Ezekiel 38-39, which tells of the threat from Gog of Magog, the foe from the north who is defeated in a cataclysmic battle. After the war is won, all nations acknowledge that God himself is the victor.

Another example is the "Isaiah Apocalypse" in Chapters 24 to 27 of Isaiah. Note especially 25:6-9 and 26:16-19 which speaks of the defeat of death and may be promising resurrection of the dead. There is some debate about the precise meaning of these passages, but they are certainly leaning in that direction and have usually been read by Christians in the light of a belief in the resurrection of the dead. Zechariah 1-8 is another example of Old Testament apocalyptic literature. The book of Revelation is the best New Testament example and is influenced by Daniel. There are also short apocalyptic passages scattered in the gospels—e.g. in Mark 13, Matthew 24, and Luke 21.

c. Persecution theme

Apocalyptic literature seems to originate in times of persecution. When the world appears hopeless and God's people are helpless to change anything, then apocalyptic makes its entrance. It is the last straw, the only place left to turn. The world makes no sense and it never will until there is some kind of divine intervention.

Only God himself has the power to remove the forces of evil which have become so entrenched in all the institutions of the world. The world is utterly decadent and there is no hope for making anything of it.

Since it comes from times of persecution, apocalyptic resembles the lament psalm in its hostility toward the enemy. The idea of dragging dead and decaying villains back to life so that they can be properly punished, not just with misfortune for this poor miserable life but for eternity, is hardly a nice thought for people who are supposed to love their enemies. There are two sides to God's justice as we perceive it. If we have not deserved what has happened to us in this world we want another chance to get what we have coming. If others have been getting away with something, then they need to get caught. The case of Hitler alone would convince many of the necessity of hell.

2. New dimensions to the meaning of suffering

Apocalyptic literature does provide some new resources for our struggle with the meaning of suffering.

Apocalyptic material puts an emphasis on cosmic evil forces separate from both God and humans. We have seen hints of this in some of the earlier Old Testament material—the snake in Genesis and Satan in Job 1-2. There are other leanings in this direction in references to God's battle with the sea monster—e.g., in Isaiah 27:1, Job 26:12-13, and Psalm 74:14. These at least imply the same kind of warfare between good and evil that emerges in the apocalyptic literature.

But apocalyptic writings carry this dualistic tendency much further. Perhaps, as many have suggested, there is some influence here from Persian dualism. There are dangers in flirting with dualism—it seems to compromise the oneness of God—but it does provide some relief from the agony of having to locate the cause of suffering in either God or ourselves. It is virtually untenable to blame God for evil, and so we get blamed for everything bad that happens in the world. With apocalyptic (as with imprecatory psalms), we have some other enemy to blame. This means that God can be on our side in the battle against suffering and evil. According to the concept of retribution, where people cause their own troubles, we are frequently put in an adversary relationship with God, constantly trying to defend ourselves from his reprisals rather than being comforted by knowing that we share a common enemy.

This way of thinking can be particularly helpful to us when the suffering is on such a grand scale that it is impossible to ascribe it to either God or to people. It is also of great benefit to sufferers who are over-scrupulous, who have turned all their misfortunes in on themselves and are wallowing in guilt. It would be less helpful for persons who already have difficulty accepting personal responsibility for their own life and are only too quick to put the blame on some outside influence—"the devil made me do it."

Apocalyptic literature has not abandoned the law of retribution, the belief that God's justice will eventually be established, that the good will be rewarded and the evil will be punished. Far from it. What has been abandoned is the effort to make it fit the experiences of *this* life. Not all the evil in this life is our fault. In fact, the world is so corrupt that the good people are more likely to suffer than the bad ones. Most of the suffering of the present age has been caused by evil forces run amok. But, as far as the *next* life is concerned, the rule of cause and effect is maintained with a vengeance.

In apocalyptic we have the beginning of an emphasis on a meaningful, identifiable, individual life after death. Other ancient religions believed in a life after death, but it seems not to have been a clear, significant tenet of belief among the ancient Hebrews. From the end of the Old Testament period, Pharisaic Judaism and then Christianity have taught a belief in new life after the grave, whether resurrection at judgment day or an immediate passage into heaven or hell. This is obviously a message of great comfort for the pious sufferer. This world is not all there is. The writer of Ecclesiastes was wrong about that. All the injustices of this world will be made right. Death does not have the final word so that even the good, well-spent, and happy life must live in fear of the oblivion that will come to all. Many would say that this is the most important answer we have to the meaning of suffering, or at least to the endurance of suffering. Many of the biblical passages that we have examined have needed a belief in a hereafter in order to give them fuller meaning. As we have looked at these texts, we almost wish that we could speak to the Old Testament writer and assure him that he need not agonize so desperately over this world because there is more to come.

Many Christians wonder how a religion can be very helpful to anyone if it does not promise a new life after this one—that is, a continuous individual existence. Our highly developed sense of individualism plus our lack of fulfillment in this life pushes us toward that attitude. We have made the fact of our own existence on into eternity the center of what must be included in a meaningful religion.

But even the great comforting truth of life after death has its problems for us. There is a price to pay for this belief—and that is the threat of eternal damnation. The retribution doctrine is not gone—its effects are merely postponed. If God is going to reward or punish us according to our merits, then we must live in fear that we will be able to pass the test. Is it better to fade away into nonexistence or to burn forever in hell? What is good news to a sufferer ("there is a better life ahead for you") may be bad news to one who has caused others suffering ("you got away with it so far, but your time will come"). Nonsufferers may worry even more than sufferers about the next life because, knowing that they are not perfect, and not having to bear many pains in this life, they may have the fear that they will have to suffer in the next world (e.g. Luke 16:25).

Since Christians believe in rewards and punishments after

death, they have devoted an enormous amount of energy specu-
lating about who gets saved and who doesn't. One wonders how
many persons have become and remained Christians out of fear
of going to hell. Many so-called evangelistic types deliberately
play on this fear in order to motivate commitments to Christianity. I am somewhat troubled by what seems to be a selfish
motivation—that is, that we love and serve God primarily because
of what rewards we will get out of it. In this context, I find myself
attracted by the implication from the prolog of Job that the only
way Job can be tested in his devotion to God is if he loses everything.

The promise of eternal bliss carries with it the threat of eternal
hell. The earlier Old Testament people had other problems (particularly when the justice of God did not appear to be at work in
the world), but they did not have to worry about burning forever
in hell. If there is a judgment after death, then the Christian needs
to know that God also forgives and is not so rigid in his need
to execute justice that he will repay us for every nasty thing we
ever did. A religion that emphasizes life after death must also
emphasize the forgiveness of sins. The message to the sufferer
is not only that there is new hope beyond this life, but also
that your sins are forgiven.

In its efforts to pronounce a hope for meaning *beyond* this life,
apocalyptic has some very negative judgments about the value
and significance of this life. If this life is only transitory, lacking
in meaning, full of suffering and evil, then the logical conclusion
is to disparage it and attempt to sail through it as uncorrupted
as possible until we get to where the real action is after we die or
experience the Second Coming. If we are always thinking how
awful the present is and see meaning only in the future, then we
have somehow thrown the biblical message out of kilter in our
efforts to provide hope for the sufferer. There certainly have
been many world-denying tendencies in the history of Christianity, and they have found support by a certain reading of the
apocalyptic literature.

We must say again that there is no single answer to the question of suffering—even though some may be tempted to say that we are finally getting close to it. There will be times when it is more appropriate to hear some other word on suffering—like the hard-nosed interpretation of the prophets who insisted that people must be obedient to God's will in this life and their behavior will have consequences in this life; or like the honest but painful realism of the lament psalm and Ecclesiastes. This is still God's creation and is not without meaning as a place where God has put us to serve him and to love him and our fellow creatures. We need to work to make this a better world—to do what we can to alleviate suffering and not ignore or belittle it because it is only temporary. The next world should be even better—but our present calling is to love and work in this one.

Apocalyptic seems most appropriate as a message for those at the end of their rope, in hopeless situations, with no place else to turn, and with this world no longer offering any solutions. So, it is a consoling word for those who are persecuted and oppressed (as it has been for prisoners in Nazi concentration camps and black slaves in the southern United States). And it is a healing word for us when we face death, when we must leave this world behind and go ahead in faith to new and better things. And it is a useful word when the evil seems so global, so cosmic, of such huge proportions that we can deal with it in no other way.

But we ought not to give in to apocalyptic answers too soon—especially not when we are still in the prime of life, when we are in positions of some influence, when we can do things to improve the world, and when there are still wonders of creation to observe and enjoy. There is a sense of inappropriateness when fascination and preoccupation with "the end of the world" emerges among middle class suburbanites, huddling together to protect themselves from a changing world. They are falling back on this "answer" too soon. When all else fails, when there is no longer anything that we can do, when we face the inevitability of death, then the apocalyptic words of hope for the future can bring a comfort that has sustained the faithful through the most terrible trials.

Apocalyptic is of most value in providing hope for the end of suffering rather than in explaining *why* the suffering happened. There is some hint of evil forces bringing it about, but that raises almost as many questions as it answers (such as, where did the devil come from if God is the Creator, why doesn't God get rid of the devil once and for all, etc.?). Apocalyptic literature is more a description of the way out of our suffering than an explanation of how we got into it.

By now, this should be familiar as a common pattern in biblical material on suffering. Over and over we have seen that God has heard the cry of pain and has promised that relief will come— even though it may not come until the next life. But the reason *why* we suffer remains a blend of several possibilities: (1) most prominently the retribution doctrine, (2) the work of some evil force, (3) for the benefit of others or ourselves, or (4) part of the divine mystery.

6

What Is New
in the
New Testament?

THE WRITERS OF THE NEW TESTAMENT knew the traditional answers to questions about the meaning of human suffering. They had their Bible, our Old Testament, and they were familiar with those same passages we have been examining. When they speak to the same persistent questions about why human beings should suffer, they have all of these ancient resources at their disposal. In this chapter we will look briefly at those Old Testament "answers" which they found most suitable to their own situations.

The most common ways of dealing with human suffering in the New Testament are inspired by Isaiah 40-55 and the apocalyptic literature. The New Testament puts a heavy emphasis on the value of suffering for the sake of others. And there is a widespread use of the apocalyptic themes of putting off judgment until the next world, the belief that the end is coming soon, the existence of cosmic evil forces, and the hope of a resurrected life after this one. These answers were particularly helpful to the early Christians who were faced with the need to explain why the long expected Messiah should have to suffer and die, and to give some explanation for the suffering of the followers of Jesus as they came in conflict with established institutions of government and religion.

There are other interpretations of suffering in the New Testament as well, most notably some vestiges of the early retribution doctrine which expected rewards and punishment in this life and the idea that suffering is actually good for the sufferer.

These ideas are not new. We have seen them already in various parts of the Old Testament. What is new in the New Testament is the way older themes are chosen and combined and filled out in their meaning by their attachment to the person of Jesus Christ. Since we have been reading the Old Testament as Christians, we have already had occasion to look ahead and remark how certain ideas would be understood at a later time. The writers of the New Testament have the Old Testament traditions to use—but they also have the story of the life, death, and resurrection of Jesus. It is their task to bring the two together. And so they search the Scriptures for those passages which best articulate what they want to say about suffering in the light of their experience of the Christ. Certain texts are deliberately chosen because they fit the story—and, in turn, the story gives the old texts a new depth and breadth which they could not have had in their original context. This is particularly true with regard to the Suffering Servant passages in Isaiah.

We shall look at examples of New Testament texts that speak to the question of meaning in suffering. We shall group them in categories which we have already established in previous chapters.

A. Reward and Punishment in This Life?

The basic biblical starting point is the belief that God is a God of justice and people will be rewarded and punished for their deeds. When this is used as a general principle and the corporate nature of society is considered, it still has some value. It even has some value on occasion within individual lives. But by the end of the Old Testament period the inclination is to give up on the possibility of individual vindication within this life, hoping that it will come in some distant eschatological or apocalyptic time. The New Testament writers would, in general, share this view. When the retribution doctrine is mentioned either directly or indirectly, the usual conclusion is that it does not work within *this* life. Nevertheless, the following texts imply that it is a persistent belief which never goes away completely in spite of all the human experience which argues against it.

Acts 5:1-11

The story of Ananias and Sapphira is very similar to stories in the early history of Israel or in the prophetic books. (One is particularly reminded of the death of Jeremiah's adversary, Hananiah, in Jeremiah 28:15-17). The historian of the early Christian church interprets the sudden death of these two people as a result of their sin—their lying to the community about their generosity. The historian of Samuel and Kings would have agreed. Those of us who are Christians and have our theology shaped by what we read in the Bible cannot help but be influenced by such texts. If God did that to sinners in those days, am I perhaps in danger that he will do it to me if I should sin? If such a calamity strikes (people drop dead from heart attacks quite often), are we to look for some cause for which a person is being punished? Most of us are prepared to argue against any universalizing of this doctrine. Yet, when we see such texts as this, it is a reminder of a belief about the meaning of suffering which never quite goes away—not in those days or in our own.

Luke 18:28-29

Peter remarks that he and the other disciples have left their homes to follow Jesus. This sacrifice that they have made will lead to some inconvenience and perhaps to some suffering. Peter seems to be asking what rewards there are for putting aside the pleasures of this life and voluntarily taking on extra difficulties. Jesus replies "that there is no man who has left house or wife or brothers or parents or children, for the sake of the kingdom of God, who will not receive manifold more in this time, and in the age to come eternal life."

According to this text, there are rewards in *this* life for the suffering we willingly undertake for the cause of the kingdom. There is also the reward of eternal life, which is promised for the followers of Jesus by all New Testament writers. But they do not all promise rewards for this life. Is Luke thinking about spiritual or emotional rewards—a feeling of oneness with God, doing good for others, having loving relationships? Such things can exist in the midst of physical suffering and material deprivation. Or is Luke promising more? Luke does seem to be more concerned with the ongoing problems of this life and less ready to move immediately into the next world than some other New Testament writers.

At any rate, this text implies that this world still makes some sense. What we do can have good or ill effects on what happens to us in *this* world, and not only in the hereafter.

Matthew 9:1-8

Here, and in other places, Jesus heals someone by pronouncing forgiveness of sins. How are we to interpret that? Does it mean that this particular person has received the affliction of paralysis because of a sin that he has committed, and that he cannot be healed until he has been forgiven? That is certainly one common way to read such texts, and again, it reinforces a belief in a retribution doctrine that affects this life. What is a sick person supposed to think? Is my illness caused by a sin? What sin was it? How can I be forgiven? Maybe I need more faith. Maybe I ought to get myself to a faith healer and give up fooling around with these medical doctors who don't seem to do any good.

Maybe Jesus is talking in a more general, symbolic way. As with Genesis 3, we can speak about sickness and suffering coming into the world as a result of human sin, and therefore we all suffer as a result of that. Jesus comes to remove that burden from us by pronouncing forgiveness of sins, and the story of the paralytic who is forgiven and achieves health is a paradigm for the salvation that awaits us all.

There are ways, such as the paragraph above, in which we try to back off from the conclusion that each sickness is a result of specific sins. For the sake of helping those who are sick, we need either to find other explanations for texts like this or to put them in a larger context with other answers to the problem of human suffering. Whatever Jesus (or the gospel writer) might have intended, many people have been led by such texts into making a direct connection between their illness and their sins.

Luke 13:1-5

This interesting text seems to argue against making conclusions about deserved suffering within this life. These unfortunate persons who got in the way of Pilate or the Siloam tower were not worse sinners than anyone else. It could have happened to anyone. So with any public disaster, an airline crash, an industrial explosion, a mine accident, we cannot say that those who were hurt or killed deserved it more than those who escaped.

But then Jesus goes on to say that unless his listeners repent they will all perish. The incidental calamities of this life cannot be explained. But sooner or later all will be held accountable (Luke probably is thinking of that in eschatological terms here) for their deeds, and without repentance there is little hope of a favorable judgment. Here we are moving more toward the dominant apocalyptic answers of the New Testament and away from the efforts to make sense out of suffering in this life.

John 9

When they came upon a man who had been blind from birth, Jesus' disciples asked him, "Rabbi, who sinned, this man or his parents, that he was born blind?" (v. 2). Jesus answered, "It was not that this man sinned, or his parents, but that the works of God might be made manifest in him" (v. 3).

This is a clear denial by Jesus that we should assume that every example of suffering is a direct result of sin, either by the individual (as in Ezekiel 18 and elsewhere) or by the ancestors of the afflicted person (as in Deuteronomy 5:9-10 and elsewhere). This is an important text to know and to use in order to balance the tendency that many people have to blame their troubles on themselves. We have no less an authority than Jesus himself to quote in this passage.

It is interesting that the disciples raise the question the way they do. It seems normal to them to assume that suffering is a result of someone's sin—though they recognize the theological debate whether an individual can be blamed for his own suffering or if we have to look into the past, either to immediate ancestors or to a more general description of the fall of the human race. Jesus bypasses both sides of that discussion and says that the blindness has nothing to do with sin at all but is an opportunity for God's glory to be seen.

In the process of denying the universal application of the retribution doctrine, we have the mention of another possible interpretation of suffering—that it exists so that God's glory can be seen in overcoming it. There is a similar idea in Exodus 10:1-2 in the explanation of why God hardened Pharaoh's heart. This idea occurs again in John 11:4, where we are told that the sickness of Lazarus is for the glory of God to be shown through the work of the Son of God. As an answer to our questions about human suffering, this would seem to be a rather limited one. It might be a good answer if you were the lucky recipient of a miracle cure so that you could "give God the glory." But if you were not relieved of your misery, you might be even more frustrated waiting for a miracle to occur. Your need would be for a text from the laments or from Job or from Paul which allows God to come into your suffering and pain and weakness and bring comfort without necessarily ending the suffering.

Matthew 5:3-12

We have been considering some vestiges of a belief in retribution within this life, but they are not a dominant part of the New Testament. The Beatitudes represent a more common New Testament conception about the connection between our fortunes in life and our piety. The Beatitudes almost completely reverse the normal expectation. The ones who are blessed are not the rich, powerful, successful, healthy, and so on. Those who are blessed are the mourners, the meek, the hungry, the poor, and those who are being persecuted for a righteous cause. (This is even more clear in Luke 6:20-26. Matthew tends to spiritualize the status of those who are blessed.) In the world of first century Christians, the good are likely to suffer more, not less, in this life. The world is so topsy-turvy that suffering, far from being a result of sin, almost becomes the sign you are one of the faithful. In such a world, the concept of retribution has meaning only as it is applied to the judgment that comes in the next life.

Most New Testament texts do not teach that the doctrine of cause and effect works in this life as an explanation for human suffering. We have pointed out a few examples where vestiges of that belief still exist and we see that it is still an option for the theologizers of that time (as Jesus' disciples with the blind man or those who wondered why the tower of Siloam fell on some men and not on others). The majority of New Testament texts, like the apocalyptic literature we looked at in the last chapter, have given up on meanings in this world and have postponed the coming of God's justice until the time when Jesus comes again or we die.

B. Suffering for the Benefit of Others

In an earlier chapter, we discussed the insight of Isaiah 40-55 that suffering can have a redemptive value for others. This idea almost surely arose as a way for Israel to find something worthwhile in the exile experience. Suffering is more than punishment. The suffering of the innocent can benefit others.

Though this is not a dominant view in the Old Testament, it becomes a dominant view in the New Testament. Isaiah 40-55, and particularly the Servant Songs, are very important texts for the New Testament writers. They helped explain why the Messiah had to suffer and they helped the new Christians understand why they, too, were called to suffer.

1. The suffering of Jesus

Why did the Messiah suffer and die? That was certainly not a common expectation among those looking for a new king to usher in a new age. What good is a dead messiah? If the messiah is supposed to bring a new world in which suffering and pain are gone forever, then what has been accomplished by the death of this man on the cross?

Those were hard questions facing those followers of Jesus who dared to believe that he was the Messiah. The cross was a liability. It was a disaster, a disgrace, a horrible climax to a promising beginning. Surely Jesus did not deserve to die. Therefore, there must have been a reason for him to die. It was for us. His death has somehow made it possible for the rest of us to escape the punishment that we would otherwise deserve. What begins as a stumbling block, an embarrassing failure, becomes a necessity in the developing theology of the church. Jesus tells the travelers to Emmaus that they are foolish and slow to believe what the prophets have written. "Was it not necessary that the Christ should suffer these things and enter into his glory?" (Luke 24: 26). In his speech in Acts 3, Peter says, "But what God foretold by the mouth of all the prophets, that his Christ should suffer, he thus fulfilled" (v. 18). The Old Testament texts that come the closest to predicting such a messiah are those in Isaiah 40-55, particularly the Servant Songs, and especially Isaiah 53.

So Jesus' suffering was for a purpose. It was for our salvation. Various theories of the atonement will attempt, with greater or lesser success, to put more intellectual content into that statement.

2. Taking up the cross

By analogy, the followers of Jesus are asked to take up their crosses and, like Jesus, suffer for the sake of spreading the gospel. We are called to suffer, as he did, and we should be willing to assume that responsibility if we are worthy to be one of his followers.

Then Jesus told his disciples, "If any man would come after me, let him deny himself and take up his cross and follow me. For whoever would save his life will lose it, and whoever loses his life for my sake will find it" (Matthew 16:24-25). In the commission to his apostles in Matthew 10:16-23, Jesus tells them to expect persecution, not (obviously) as a result of their sins but as a direct consequence of bringing the message of Christ to a sinful world.

In the epistles we find many such exhortations to the people to be faithful in spite of the suffering that will be required of them. In 2 Corinthians 11:16—12:10, Paul, in a rather immodest way, recites a litany of sufferings which he has endured for the cause, with the implication that his readers ought to be willing to do likewise and with the assurance that God's strength is best shown in our own weakness. In the letter to the Philippians, Paul puts the best possible interpretation on his experience of suffering in prison. He believes that his ordeal in prison has helped others and the spread of the gospel (1:12-14). He calls it a privilege to be able to suffer for Christ and encourages his readers to look on their own suffering in the same way (1:29-30). In 2 Timothy, the reader is admonished to be a good soldier and suffer for the cause of Christ. Similar advice is given in Hebrews 12 and 1 Peter 2.

Suffering is to be expected as the normal outcome for one who makes a firm commitment to Christ. Just as Jesus met a hostile world when he spoke his message, so will be the fate of Jesus' followers when they speak those same words. They should not be surprised when they suffer, even if they suffer when they have not deserved it.

This is a dominant theme in the New Testament, conditioned by the suffering of Jesus, the difficult times facing the followers of Jesus in the early days of the church, and the ideas provided by the ancient prophet in Isaiah 40-55.

There are problems if we try to apply this meaning of suffering too broadly. Can we say that most human suffering has a potential value for others? Does experience bear that out? We have looked at this in some detail in a previous chapter and will not raise that whole discussion again. Suffice it to say that this was a comforting word from God to the followers of Jesus at a time when they were called upon to take heroic stands for the sake of the gospel. How suited is it to our own day, when it seems to be more difficult to find a way to suffer for the faith? Perhaps with a proper sense of servanthood, we could find ways to bring our faith into actions that would indeed bring us more suffering. That is an important aspect of the value of this text for us. But it is a fact that most of our sufferings, unlike those of first century Christians, have nothing to do with our commitment to the faith. The idea of suffering for others, for some greater cause, in some noble mission will not provide much insight for ordinary sufferings which come into our lives unannounced and unasked for ("we didn't volunteer for any mission") and do not appear to have potential benefit for anyone.

C. The Answers of Apocalyptic Thinking

As we saw in the last chapter, apocalyptic literature grew out of a time when expectations for this world were very dismal. Apocalyptic answers to the question of suffering are most appropriate for those who are in the midst of great suffering, persecution, and the danger of death. These answers show little concern with the present. Rather, they focus the attention of the sufferer on the glorious future, the time when all will be made right and all suffering and evil will cease. By concentrating on that hope, the sufferer is able to endure the unpleasantness of the present.

The apocalyptic answers emerge at the end of the Old Testament period. Some of them (such as the belief in a resurrection) are the appropriate development of a long-felt need. These ideas about the meaning of suffering are very important throughout the New Testament, where they find a much fuller expression than in the Old Testament literature.

Let us look again at some of the ideas about suffering from the apocalyptic literature and see how they are applied in the New Testament.

1. The world to come

God's vindication will come—but in the next world, not this one. This world makes no sense any more. But God is still a God of justice and will reward the good people and punish the bad. The good people who are suffering in this life will get their rewards in the next life—and the evil ones who are enjoying luxury in this world had better get all they can get out of it, because they are in for big trouble in the life to come (e.g., the parable of the rich man and Lazarus in Luke 16:19-31).

Many texts speak about rewards and punishments in the next life on the basis of how we live in this life. In the Sermon on the Mount, Jesus speaks of rewards for those who do the will of God. Not one iota of the law is to be relaxed (Matthew 5:17-

20), God will reward us for the good we do in secret (Matthew 6:3-4), and it is not enough just to call "Lord, Lord" without doing the will of God (Matthew 7:21-24). On judgment day, all people will be held accountable for their words (Matthew 12:36-37). There are many references to poor souls who are to be cast into outer darkness amid weeping and gnashing of teeth (e.g., Matthew 25:30) or thrown into hell (as in Matthew 5:27-30). In the great judgment scene in Matthew 25:31-46, the sheep and the goats are separated with some gaining eternal life and the others going into eternal punishment, on the basis of how they have acted toward their fellow human beings. The book of Revelation has many clear references to a final judgment in which everyone will be repaid for what they have done, with some entering eternal bliss and some thrown into a lake of fire (Revelation 20:13-15). "Behold, I am coming soon, bringing my recompense, to repay everyone for what he has done" (Revelation 22:12).

This belief in a judgment after death may be a comfort to the sufferer. It provides the hope of vindication in a later life in the absence of justice in this life. This world is not the only place where God's justice can have its sway. If my life is miserable and I suffer at the hands of evil persons, it is a great comfort to know that that is not the end of the matter. There may even be a good chance to vent hostility toward my oppressors by imagining the suffering that will come their way when they finally get what is coming to them.

But there is a darker side to this word of hope. If such a judgment is coming, then we are all in danger of suffering in the next life also. If there is a hell, then someone is probably going to be sent there, and since no one is perfect, we are all in danger of burning in an eternal fire. So, the belief in a final judgment may actually cause us additional suffering, as we are in great anxiety about our own worthiness to pass the final test when the book of life is opened (Revelation 20:12-15). Paul was particularly bothered by this possibility. In Romans 2:1-11, he grants that we will all be judged by what we do. God's justice demands it. He goes on in Romans 3 to say that we are all sinners and fall short of the glory of God (3:23). No one can keep the law so we are all condemned. The only way we can be put right with God is by faith in Jesus Christ, being justified by God's grace as a gift, through the redemption which is in Christ Jesus. For Paul (and some other texts could be included, such as John 3:36 and John 12:44-50), the crucial ingredient in our final judgment will not be our deeds (we would all fail on that count) but whether or not we have faith in the Lord Jesus Christ. If we have such faith, we will survive the last judgment and find eternal joy rather than eternal punishment.

So, there is to be a final judgment. This life does not have the last word. But will we be among those who deserve heaven? We have pointed out two ways of dealing with this question in the New Testament. One (as in the quotes from Matthew and Revelation) puts the emphasis on our willingness to be obedient to God's will and to serve our neighbor. On that basis we will be judged. The other (as in Paul and John) is more pessimistic about getting a favorable judgment on our activity and sees our only hope in attaching ourselves to Jesus in faith because he has taken on himself the punishment that is rightfully ours. The former view believes that good works are crucial. The latter view believes that no works are good enough and throws us back on God's grace.

Does the thought of vindication in the next life help or hinder the sufferer? It certainly brings many crucial theological questions with it. In particular, it raises the need to be assured that we will be one of those upon whom God looks favorably—otherwise we may be suffering not only for three score years and ten but for eternity.

2. Cosmic evil forces

There is much talk about cosmic evil forces in the New Testament. In the gospels, there are many indications that demons of

one kind or another cause illness and Jesus casts out the demons in order to make a person well. Jesus is tempted by Satan
(in Mark) or the devil (in Matthew and Luke) at the beginning
of his ministry. When Judas, one of the closest followers of Jesus
and chosen by the Master himself, turned betrayer, at least a
partial reason is given in the idea that Satan had influenced him
(Luke 22:3 and John 13:27). Paul frequently talks about Satan
as a near and constant threat, as do other epistle writers (e.g., 1
John 3:7-12 and 5:18-19 and 1 Peter 5:8). In Revelation 20, the
final conflict with the devil (dragon, serpent, Satan) is described
in some detail.

As an explanation of suffering and evil, this idea is not central
to the Old Testament. It becomes very prominent in the New
Testament. It helps us explain some manifestations of evil, but
also brings some problems of its own—such as God's willingness
to allow such forces in opposition to himself if he is powerful
enough to subdue them, temptations to elevate the devil to the
status of a god, and the tendency to blame Satan for the wrong
we do rather than to assume our own responsibility.

In the days when I was in seminary, we tended to look on the
stories of casting out demons as a rather primitive way of understanding physical and mental illness. It was thought that we
should simply dismiss such language as a pre-scientific understanding of the origin of certain phenomena which can now be
better explained by things like bacteria, viruses, and unhappy
childhoods. In recent years, there seems to be more inclination by
some to take these biblical passages at their face value. Perhaps
there are some cases of suffering which have not yet been explained in any better way.

3. The resurrection of the dead

Jesus himself, like the Pharisees, believed in a resurrection of
the dead (as shown in his argument with the Sadduccees in
Mark 12:18-27 and parallels in Matthew and Luke). In the

Synoptic gospels he speaks only occasionally about the life after death, but there are more such words in John. This belief had already emerged at the end of the Old Testament period and was carried forth into Judaism by the Pharisees. In Christianity, however, it assumes great significance because of its connection with Jesus' resurrection. As Christ has been raised to new life, so also will his followers be raised to new life.

Some of the important texts on the belief in a resurrection are John 11:25, Acts 4:2, 1 Corinthians 15, Philippians 1:20-26, 1 Thessalonians 4:13-18, and Revelation 20:11-15. These are passages which are very helpful to the sufferer, particularly at the time when one's own death is approaching or when we have lost a loved one. A belief in a meaningful life after death has been central to Christianity from the beginning and, as we have noted earlier, was one of the things missing from most Old Testament answers to the problem of suffering. We are reminded, however, that when a heavy emphasis is laid on the judgment that will take place after death, then this message of hope can bring new problems. We need God's assurance, through his Son, that our sins are forgiven and we do not have to fear either death or what comes after.

4. The Second Coming

In the early days of the church, the expectation was that Christ would return before long and remedy all the ills of the world. Though not all New Testament literature is apocalyptic, the mood of the time was certainly one of apocalyptic anticipation. We can see this most clearly in the apocalyptic passages, such as Revelation, Matthew 24, Mark 13, and Luke 21. The signs are all around. The end cannot be far off. Those who are suffering for the cause of Jesus Christ should be encouraged by their suffering. One of the signs of the end is the suffering of the faithful so, in a real sense, the more we suffer the closer we are to final deliverance. Rather than be disheartened by persecution, ridicule, alienation from society, and the death of some community leaders, the true believers should find strength in the knowledge that their own pain is one of the indications that the bad things will soon be removed forever.

This must have been a comforting word to many in those days. Most of us these days think of the Second Coming as something rather remote (to say the least) and we expect that our entrance into a new age will come after our death and not before. Therefore, we would not be much comforted by the idea that the worse things get, the more they indicate the rapid approach of the end of the world. Perhaps if things get bad enough (air pollution, no more oil, terrorism, corrupt politicians, declining morality, and so on), we may have more and more people finding comfort again in this apocalyptic vision of the final days.

D. Other New Testament Texts on Human Suffering

The idea of suffering for others and the various answers developed from the apocalyptic literature are the most prominent ways of dealing with suffering in the New Testament. There are some other texts, however, which should be noted briefly.

There are some passages which express a hope for the future in such beautiful and meaningful words that they have been a comfort to Christians throughout the ages. In some ways they are like the most beautiful prophetic passages of the Old Testament in their longing for a new day when all the sorrow and pain of the present will be gone. Though we Christians have seen Christ, we still wait, with our Old Testament ancestors, for the final fulfillment of all our hopes and aspirations. We wait for the Second Coming because we know that the world is still not the way it should be.

In John 16:19-24, Jesus comforts his followers with the promise that, even though they will experience sadness and the need to lament for a time, he will see them again and their sorrow will be transformed into the greatest joy. Romans 8:18-39 is a lovely word of hope. The sufferings of the present time are not worth comparing with the glory that will be shown at a later time. There is no evil strong enough to hurt us for God is for us. In 1 Peter 5:6-11, we are told to humble ourselves before God in the sure knowledge that, in due time, he will exalt us. Revelation 7:16-17 and 21:4 speak of a time when there will no longer be hunger or thirst and God will be there to wipe away every tear.

I have found all of these passages to be very helpful words from God to people who are suffering.

The idea that suffering can be good for people was not a major theme in the Old Testament, but we did find it in the Book of Job and other places. It also appears in the New Testament and has been a rather common explanation for suffering (at least some suffering) throughout the history of the church. There is a certain appeal to this view. We all know occasions when, at least with hindsight, it has seemed to work. We are better persons for the refining, the discipline, the rebuilding of character which has taken place because of our personal suffering.

Romans 5:1-5 is often quoted as an explanation for suffering. "Suffering produces endurance, and endurance produces character and character produces hope," and so on. In 2 Corinthians 7:8-11, Paul recognizes that he caused some unhappiness because of a critical letter which he had written earlier. But he does not regret having written it and thereby causing them some discomfort because their suffering over the letter brought them to repentance. The suffering was good for them. Paul had disciplined them as a father must sometimes discipline his children. This idea is stated very clearly in Hebrews 12:5-11, beginning with a quote from Proverbs 3:11-12 which makes the same point. The discipline which we endure seems painful for a time, but later yields its good fruits. 1 Peter 1:7-9 puts a slightly different slant on the idea that suffering is good for us by pointing out that our trials are for the purpose of testing our faith. (One is reminded of the prolog to the Book of Job.)

This line of reasoning may be helpful to certain people at certain times as they attempt to understand the suffering in their lives. But the counselor must beware of turning these wise sayings into platitudes that are spoken off the top of the head without first probing the depths with the sufferer. Like Job's counselors, we may be guilty of misapplying words that (though helpful in another context) do not speak to the one who is in need of comfort, and, in fact, may even prove harmful.

E. Conclusions

What the New Testament says about the meaning of suffering was already there by the end of the Old Testament. Most of the explanations for the existence of evil and suffering had already been tried, though in the case of apocalyptic, the development had not proceeded very far by the end of the Old Testament period. When we are looking for intellectual answers to our questions of why people suffer, there is not much that is new in the New Testament.

What is "new" is the person of Jesus Christ. The older traditional answers to the questions of meaning in suffering are now influenced by the story of the death and resurrection of Jesus. And so there is a powerful appeal to those Old Testament passages that speak of the suffering for others and the possibilities of life after death. Though these ideas are present in the Old Testament, they are not yet associated with the Person whom God sent. When it is God himself who suffers for us and with us on the cross, then the implications of Isaiah 53 are far more profound than anyone could have guessed. When the risen Christ confronts his followers and turns them from frightened victims of despair to fearless messengers of the faith, then the hope of life after death takes on a vividness and power that it could not have before.

We still have trouble understanding the "why" of our suffering, and the New Testament has little to add here. But we have added much on the spiritual, survival level. Our God knows our pain because he has been there with us. We live in the hope that, eventually, he will take the suffering away. In the meantime, we know that we have a God who weeps with us, who hears and understands our cries of pain, who is completely approachable even when we walk through the valley of the shadow of death. To believe in such a God is enough.

The books of the New Testament, as the rest of the Bible, are written to specific life-situations. The texts on human suffering are addressed to those who expect the world to end soon, who are powerless to bring any real improvement to their own status or that of the world around them, and who are called upon to make extreme sacrifices for their faith in the hope of rewards in the hereafter. If our situation is like that one, then there is a good chance that the special emphasis of the New Testament books will be of great value to us in finding meaning in our suffering.

But what if that does not adequately describe the present state of my world? Perhaps I am one who is so moved by the suffering of this world that I am not willing to be put off by the promise of a new world. What if I think that something should be done now and that present suffering is intolerable even if it may seem a small thing in the perspective of eternity? What if I like this life and want to affirm its beauty and opportunities for loving relationships and responsibilities and creativity? The world did not come to a quick end, removing all human suffering once and for all, as many New Testament writers expected. If we limit our search for meaningful texts on suffering to the New Testament, we will be confined to passages addressed to situations that may be much different from our own. There may be other texts which speak more directly to the skeptic, the worldly person, the one who has never been called on to suffer for a cause, the one who does not expect the world to end within the lifetime of this or the next generation, the one who needs to lament a bit longer before settling for any "too easy" solution.

In short, we still need the entire Bible. There remains no single biblical answer to the question of meaning in suffering. God has led us to preserve all of Scripture, with its variety of comforting messages for all kinds of people in all kinds of circumstances. God comes to us whatever our need, with a word that will help us understand, or at least endure, our suffering.

7

Comfort and Hope

WHAT DOES THE BIBLE SAY about the meaning of human suffering? That was our starting point. As Christians, we assumed that the Bible must have answers for us as we try to understand and endure the sufferings that come to our lives. As we have moved through the Scripture, we have found that the Bible says many things about human suffering. We have looked at texts from Genesis to Revelation. At certain points in the history of God's people, such as the time of Judah's exile or the persecutions of the early church, the question was very close to the surface and the biblical writers were concerned to provide words from God to sustain the sufferer.

In this concluding chapter, I shall attempt to put the biblical answers in perspective by highlighting the themes that have consistently recurred throughout our study. First, I shall summarize the various answers to the question of meaning in suffering. Second, I shall comment on some implications for those who would bring comfort to those who suffer.

A. Summary: What the Bible Says About Suffering

The Bible deals with suffering on two levels: the intellectual level—the search for reasons *why* there is suffering in the world and *why* it comes to some and not to others; and the survival level—the effort to provide support and comfort to the person who is experiencing suffering. The two approaches are not mutually exclusive, but there are occasions when one is more appropriate than the other. The intellectual approach is most fitting for the times in our lives when we have some breathing space, when there is no immediate painful crisis to bear, when we can look with some objectivity on past experience and anticipate our future, when the suffering of the world has not struck so close to home that our thoughts are distorted and our despair is engulfing. The survival approach is for those times when the present suffering so preoccupies our mind and soul that we can see little else and we need a glimmer of hope to give us the strength to go on.

We will summarize the answers to suffering in two groups, corresponding to the two levels of approach in the Bible.

1. The intellectual level: rational answers

a. It is our own fault

The concept of retribution in one form or another, is the most common biblical explanation for the presence of evil and suffering. God is not responsible for the suffering that is so much a part of life in the world. Human beings are. This view protects God's good name by blaming human beings for all the bad things. Even when God becomes angry and causes evil to come upon us, it is because of something we have done to encourage that reaction. According to this view, human beings must bear the burden for all the troubles of this world.

When stated in a general way, as descriptive of the corruption that came to God's good creation because of human sin, this view is still a very dominant one. All people are sinners, and therefore the world is full of suffering—it has been so since the time of Adam and it remains so to the present.

Stated in those terms, however, it is not much help in explaining why some suffer more than others. If all are sinners, then why are not all suffering? Some biblical writers attempt to be more precise in applying this doctrine to specific events in the history of the people and even to specific events in the lives of individuals. And so we read that Israel went into exile because of the sin of Jeroboam, Hananiah and Ananias died because of their sins of lying, and we will be blessed if we obey the law and cursed if we do not. From these and similar passages we have learned to interpret suffering in our life as a sign that we have done something for which we should be punished.

By the time we get to the end of the Old Testament period and into the New Testament, many have given up on the idea of applying the law of retribution with such confidence to the misfortunes of this life. But the idea of retribution has not been discarded. If there is not justice here, then it will come in the next world. The individual sufferings of this age may not be the result of sin—it becomes difficult to maintain that view, especially at a time when the good people are being persecuted. In the next world, however, all individuals will be rewarded or punished as they deserve. God is a God of justice and will vindicate the innocent and punish the guilty.

All of these answers to the problem of suffering are related— from the general to the more specific application, from the necessity of seeing it work in *this* life to the opening up of the time of resolution to some far distant or apocalyptic times. The story of the fall, the prophetic injunctions to obey or else, the interpretations by the historians, and the apocalyptic vision of a final judgment all share the belief that the world is suffering because of human sin. They differ from each other with regard to the legitimacy of interpreting the suffering of *individuals* within *this* life as the result of sin.

b. God will make good come out of our suffering

This explanation of suffering is not necessarily in contradiction to the idea that we bring our sufferings on ourselves. Sometimes the two go together. As with Isaiah 40-55, you can say that some of our suffering is a result of our sin, but the excess of what we deserve can have some positive effects for others. Similarly, I may not actually deserve the suffering I am experiencing, but it will make me a better person. That at least implies some defects in my character which will be improved by this refining process, and that is not so far removed from the idea that I deserved the suffering.

We have seen two main directions in which this answer moves. My suffering may be of benefit to others or it may be of benefit to myself. It is conceivable that it could benefit both others and myself, though that need not be so.

This answer depends a great deal on the attitude of the sufferer, a willingness to see God's presence even in unpleasant events, and a desire to make the most out of whatever life brings. This is an answer that works best with hindsight, looking back on sufferings that have already been endured and seeing how they have affected our life for the better. It is an answer that is rarely of much comfort during the depths of suffering unless the suffering is a result of the acceptance of a noble mission.

c. Suffering comes from evil forces

This answer to the why of suffering, though it does not develop very fully until the end of the Old Testament period, has become a very common one in Christianity. But even though there is a devil, a Satan, and demonic forces to influence us toward wrongdoing, we are still responsible for what we do and must pay the price for disobedience to God's will. The excuse that "the devil made me do it" is not good enough. No matter what the pressure on us and no matter where it comes from, we are still responsible for our own lives and must answer for what we have done.

On the other hand, there are times when it is a help to recognize that there is an evil force that wants us to suffer. Suffering may come from a source other than God or ourselves, and we can join with God in the battle against a common enemy.

d. Suffering is a mystery

There are some things that we cannot know. We are only created beings; we are not God. We ask questions the wrong way. We expect one kind of answer, and God gives another. Habakkuk wants to know why the Babylonians get off free while God's own people have to suffer. God says "Wait, and trust me." Job demands to know why he is suffering, and God tells him that he has no possibility of knowing things like that when he doesn't even understand the elementary facts of life about creation. Paul begs to have his thorn in the flesh removed and receives the word that God's power is shown in our weakness.

We cannot penetrate God's mystery. This, too, is an explanation of human suffering, even though its effect is to cut off the search for further answers. Many Christians will use one of the other explanations as long as they work, but, when all else fails, they will fall back on the idea that it is all part of God's mystery and we can never know more than that. Certainly, there are limits to our human efforts to understand God and the universe, but we ought not abandon the search too soon. There are some things we can say before we fall back on a plea of ignorance.

2. The survival level: comfort and hope for the sufferer

If, in fact, we can never penetrate the mysteries of God's work in the world, if there is no answer that works all the time, if even our best hypothesis for understanding why humans suffer crumbles when we are called to suffer, then what are we to do? We are asked to endure our times of suffering without knowing why it is happening to us.

But we are not left comfortless. There are ways in which the Bible provides us a process to help us endure. There are passages that are less concerned with the *why* of suffering than with the *how* of suffering.

a. Negative feelings should be expressed

It is a cruel thing to take away a person's right to lament. In a world like ours, with its pain and suffering and inevitability of death, the least one should be permitted to do is to complain when suffering comes. Lamenting should be a natural part of our human existence—a reasonable and appropriate response to unpleasant things that happen to us. And yet, many do not feel that it is proper for them to express negative feelings. They think they should bear their sufferings like good soldiers. They should look inward for reasons why they are having a bad time. They should look on suffering as a positive thing—a way to bring good to others and/or strengthen their own character. Passages that encourage a suppression of lament are quoted in our churches all the time. The laments themselves are ignored, carefully edited, and considered to be unworthy for those whose faith is really strong.

Suffering is real. It is unpleasant. One should not be asked to deny it. We need to recover for the church the ability to bring our complaints before God, knowing that we will have a hearing, knowing that we are not expected to have everything in good order when we cry out in pain, and knowing that God accepts us as we are. The God who sent his Son to die for us is not oblivious to our suffering. He is not defensive even when we lash out in anger at him for allowing us such pain. God has taken our sorrows and suffering and guilt upon himself. He will walk through the darkest valleys with us. Therefore we need to let go of our fear that our true thoughts and feelings will not be acceptable to him and that he will respond in anger at our foolishness and blasphemy. Many who need to lament but are afraid to do so find great comfort when they discover those parts of the Bible that allow them to say out loud what has been lying secretly within their hearts.

There is a common theme in the cries of the Hebrew slaves in Egypt, the confessions of the prophet Jeremiah, the lament psalm, Job's fierce struggle to maintain his integrity, and the cries of Jesus from the cross. Even Ecclesiastes could be included, with its realistic analysis of the vanity of all things human and its willingness to speak bluntly about the world. "For everything there is a season, and a time for every matter under heaven... a time to weep, and a time to laugh; a time to mourn, and a time to dance" (Ecclesiastes 3:1, 4).

b. Wait—in the assurance that relief is coming

Again and again the sufferer is promised that God has heard, that suffering is not the normal state of existence, that God will win a victory over pain and evil. All through the Bible, those who are suffering possess the hope that there will be an end to the bad things of life. Habakkuk is told to be patient—God will work it out in good time. The singer of the lament psalm knows that God will act to bring relief. Job has his fortunes restored even more than before. Israel is promised a return from exile, a new king, unimaginable prosperity, and unending peace. When the world becomes too corrupt and evil to see any hope for removal of the suffering, then the time of vindication is moved further away, to the distant future, or to a new world that will come when Jesus returns or when we individually pass through death to new life.

Whatever the cause of the present suffering, a person is assured that it will end one day. God is present and he cares. There is reason to hope, and hope can sustain a person through the worst possible kind of suffering.

But how much can we promise? And how soon do we interrupt a lament to speak with optimism about a time of deliverance? In the midst of despair or grief or pain, it is very difficult to have any hope at all. The present seems to be a pit or a dead end street with no possible way of escape. Nothing can be seen beyond the immediate torment. A word of hope that is spoken too soon, too glibly, even out of the most urgent motivation to be of help, may appear to the sufferer as a meaningless platitude spoken by one who has never known what real suffering is. We have a word of hope, to be sure, and that hope makes suffering bearable. But we cannot rush it. Perhaps there needs to be more time for lamenting, without any false or premature assurances, before one is finally prepared to hear God's promise of victory.

We cannot promise too much. For this life, we cannot promise recovery of health, healing of broken relationships, a lifetime without anxiety, or any way to avoid the final fact of death. Someone who is suffering from fear of death may actually be about to die, and our knee-jerk defensive assurances that "everything will be all right" are neither honest nor helpful. They perhaps save us from the unpleasant task of walking closely through another's pain—but we are called to bear one another's suffering, not to avoid it.

We have a word of hope. We know a God who hears our cry for help, and who will win the final victory over all things that hurt us. How all that will work out in the life of each sufferer is not for us to know. All we can do is to help persons bring their burdens to God, and then trust God's promises that the Holy Spirit will work within that process to bring them comfort and make hope a reality.

c. God hears and cares

For many sufferers, there comes a point when they do believe that God has heard, that he cares, and that there is a possibility of getting out of their present situation. Somehow, their faith has survived and, perhaps, it has even been strengthened. The psalmist stops singing the blues and begins to praise. Job realizes that God loves him and he is no longer weighted down by all his unanswered questions. Peter and John and the rest know that Jesus is alive.

God shows himself in the midst of suffering. Sometimes it takes a long time. There is no way to control when and how it will happen. Job wanted an audience with God, but it took many chapters before it came, suddenly, out of the whirlwind. We look for signs, miracle cures, some evidence that God is around and that he cares. Our faith is so flimsy and the questions raised by our suffering push it to the breaking point. Some sufferers lose their faith before any assurance comes. That tragedy is hard to accept. Others find that their faith becomes more certain—and, as that happens, their need for rational explanations for their suffering fades into the background.

Faith is an elusive thing. It cannot be programmed. There is nothing we can do to make it happen, or even to prevent its occurrence. Faith is the ultimate answer to the question of suffering, but we humans cannot bring about faith in anyone. Only God can do that. We can try to remove as many barriers and open as many doors as possible between God and the sufferer so that the Holy Spirit is not impeded in its work. We can share our own faith as far as we understand it. We can make available those biblical resources through which God has promised to give insight and strength. But we cannot make another person believe. Sometimes it happens and sometimes it doesn't.

B. Giving Comfort to Those Who Suffer

Each biblical answer to the question of suffering has some value, but also brings its own problems. Often, a new biblical word came as a corrective in order to balance the misuse of a previous word. For example, the belief in retribution was adapted and changed and even denied because new situations made the old interpretations no longer helpful, and even harmful. Since all of our answers to the "why" of human suffering are only partial, contextual, penultimate, they can never explain every example of human suffering. Though each answer can have value for a certain person and time and place, each may also bring problems because the mysteries of suffering cannot be contained in a single intellectual proposition.

Many times in this study we have pointed out the strengths and weaknesses of a particular way of dealing with human suffering. We have tried to indicate what life situations are more or less appropriate to a specific answer.

Part of our role as comforters is to protect sufferers from biblical answers that could be harmful to them, or at least not as helpful as some other passages would be. This means that we are to comfort sufferers not by shielding them from certain parts of Scripture but by showing the rich variety of biblical words available to them. Our view of Scripture is usually too narrow. We need to help people discover the many biblical passages that can speak appropriately to their own situations. This means that we may sometimes find ourselves arguing against some things that are found in the Bible—using one passage as a balance or corrective against another. This may disturb some people who imagine that the Bible speaks only one message—even on a subject as complicated as human suffering. That kind of narrow understanding of Scripture is part of the problem for sufferers who seek answers in the Bible.

If we are to be of any help to those who are suffering, we need to develop our own understanding of the "why" of human suffering. You cannot walk with another through profound suffering if you have not prepared yourself by coming to some clear views of your own. We all need to think this subject through so that we are not caught by surprise when confronted by intense suffering.

We may borrow some of the biblical answers. We may select those answers that seem to work best for us. At any rate, we do need some reasonable answers, however temporary they may be, in order to make sense out of the world. There is an important intellectual task here that ought not be abandoned.

The danger is to be so satisfied with our own system for explaining human suffering that we begin to apply it in more general and universal ways. I will want to share with you something that has been helpful to me. But when I am counseling you at a time of suffering, I must be cautious in speaking of my solution until I have given you the time to say what you think and feel. What I have devised as beneficial for me may not be right for you, and I must resist the temptation to force you to accept my favorite explanations of suffering.

When we are attempting to comfort one who is suffering, our first priority should be to strengthen his or her faith and not to give pat answers. Our desire for those who suffer is to sustain and strengthen their faith in God so that their suffering can be borne, hope can be seen, and the presence of God can be felt. There are no easy ways to do that. As we have said, it is beyond human power to instill faith in any one. And yet, the kinds of answers we give and the way we communicate with the sufferer may have some influence on that person's faith. For example, if we want to tell a sufferer about a God who hears the cry of distress and is moved by it, then it certainly helps our case if we are able to listen to the lament and not give in to the impulse to run from the pain or shut off the complaint or respond too quickly with pious platitudes.

As comforters of those who suffer we should be primarily concerned with keeping open the communications between the sufferer and God. We know that we cannot provide convincing answers by ourselves. God can and will answer for himself. And our own faith is put to the test by our willingness to allow the deepest painful questions to be asked and by our confidence that God indeed will respond.

There is suffering in the world. We have answers that help, but they are partial. Faith, after all, is not faith any more if it is certainty. We believe, and yet we do not. We lament, and yet we hope. We die, and yet we live. God has sent us words to help us understand and endure our sufferings. He has sent us his Son so that we may know what kind of a God he is and so that we may find it easier to believe, even in the midst of suffering. In times of trial, we, like our biblical ancestors, may wish for more. But what he has given us is enough.

"My grace is sufficient for you, for my power is made perfect in weakness" (2 Corinthians 12:9).

Index
of Biblical Passages

OLD TESTAMENT

Genesis
1-2 22
3 ....22ff., 84, 117, 127
4-11 23
50:15-21 .... 74f.

Exodus
10:1-2 128
20:5-6 .... 24f.
34:6-7 .... 24f., 34

Numbers
14:18 .... 24f.

Deuteronomy 33, 35
5:9-10 .... 24f., 128
5:11, 16 25
8:1-6 92

24:16 30
27 25
28 25
28:35 .... 26, 89
30:15-20 .... 26, 38

Joshua 27
7 27

Judges 27, 33
2:6-23 27

Samuel 27

Kings 27

2 Kings
17 .... 28, 106
17:7 28

1 Chronicles
21 84

Job 81ff., 102, 129, 147
1-2 .... 85f., 117, 120
1:8 .... 83, 109, 114
4:7-8 89
4:17 89
5:7 90
5:17 91
7:20 92
9:22-24 92
13:1-13 93
20:4-5 90
23:3-7 93
26:12-13 117
32-37 .... 82, 94
36:9-12, 15 91
38ff. .... 93ff.
38 83
42:5-6 95
42:7-17 ....86f.

Lament psalms . 44, 55ff., 87, 98,
109, 121, 148

Psalms
6:5 47
6:6-7, 11 49
17:1-2 50
22:1 .... 47, 79
23 18
25:6-7, 11 49
38:3-5, 18 49
44:17 50
44:23-24 47
51:1-12 49
58:6-8 .... 45f.
69:1-2 56
74:14 117
88:9-12 47
130 49

137:9 46

Proverbs
3:11-12 139
25:20 59

Ecclesiastes . 103, 105ff., 119, 121
1:2 107
2:14-16 107
2:18-19 108
2:24-25 109
3:1, 4 149
3:12-13 109
3:19-20 108
3:22 109
5:18-20 109
8:14 108
8:15 109
8:17 107
9:2 108
9:4-5 108
9:10 109
9:11 108
12:8 107
12:9-14 107

Isaiah 28
2:2-4 111
2:4 112
7:14 113
9:6-7 113
11:1-5 113
11:1-9 111
11:6-9 112
24-27 116
25:6-9 116
26:16-19 116
27:1 117
40-55 ...... 65ff., 84, 92, 106,
123, 130ff., 146
40:1-2 69
40:27-28 66

42:1-4 69
42:6 69
42:18-22 67
42:24-25 .... 67f.
43:9-10 69
43:24b 68
47:1-3 .... 66f.
47:6 68
48:17-19 68
49:1-6 69
49:4 67
49:6 69
49:14-15 67
50:1 68
50:4-9 69
50:7-9 71
52:13—53:12 69
53 .... 79, 131, 140
53:4-6 77
53:10-12 71

Jeremiah's Confessions . 44, 53ff.,
                               109

Jeremiah 77
11:18—12:6 .... 54ff.
15:10-21 .... 54f.
15:10b-11 50
15:18 47
17:14-18 .... 54f.
17:18 45
18:18-23 .... 54f.
20:7-12 .... 54f.
20:14-18 .... 54f.
28:15-17 125
31:29-30 30
31:31-34 111
31:31, 33b 112
33:14-18 .... 111, 113

Ezekiel ...... 29, 33, 36f., 40f.
18 ...... 29ff., 41, 77, 89, 100,
                      106, 128

18:4 30
18:20 30
18:30-32 38
38-39 .... 104f., 116

Daniel 104f., 116
12:1-2 116

Hosea 28

Amos 28, 33
2:6-7, 13-16 28
4:11-12 28
5:14-15 28
6:14 28
9:11-15 111
9:13 112

Micah 28
4:1-4 111
4:3b-4 .... 104f.
5:2-4 .... 111, 113

Habakkuk 44 90, 94, 114,
                       147, 149
1:1—2:4 .... 44, 51ff.
1:2, 13 47

Zechariah 84
1-8 116

NEW TESTAMENT

Matthew
5:3-12 .... 129f.
5:17-20 133
5:27-30 134
6:3-4 134
7:21-24 134
9:1-8 .... 126f.
10:16-23 131
12:36-37 134

16:24-25 131
24 .... 116, 137
25:30 134
25:31-46 134

Mark
12:18-27 136
13 .... 116, 137

Luke
6:20-26 .... 129f.
13:1-5 .... 127f.
16:19-31 133
16:25 119
18:28-29 .... 125f.
21 .... 116, 137
22:3 136
24:26 131

John
3:36 135
9 .... 128f.
11:4 128
11:25 137
12:44-50 135
13:27 136
16:19-24 138

Acts
3 131
4:2 137
5:1-11 125

New Testament Epistles ... 49

Romans
2:1-11 134
3 135
5:1-5 139
8:18-39 139

1 Corinthians
15 137

2 Corinthians
7:8-11 139
11:16—12:10 131
12:9 154

Philippians
1:12-14 .... 131f.
1:20-26 137
1:29-30 132

1 Thessalonians
4:13-18 137

2 Timothy 132

Hebrews
12 132
12:5-11 139

1 Peter
1:7-9 139
2 132
2:19-25 65
5:6-11 139
5:8 136

1 John
3:7-12 136
5:18-19 136

Revelation 104f., 116, 137
7:16-17 139
20 136
20:11-15 137
20:12-15 134
20:13-15 134
21:4 139
22:12 134